On the Road in the Hundred Years War

Tales from Froissart Volume 1

STONEBUNNY PRESS

On the Road in the Hundred Years War
Copyright © 2016 Steven Muhlberger

Published by Stonebunny Press
195 Drew Street, Oshawa, ON, L1H 5A4, Canada

Book design by Todd H. C. Fischer
Cover created by Todd Fischer and Melanie Fischer
Cover image is The Battle of Crecy, from Chapter
CXXIX of Jean Froissart's Chronicles,
courtesy Wikimedia Commons.
Interior images courtesy Wikimedia Commons
Title font is Charlemagne Std
Interior title font is Baskerville Old Face
Interior font is Book Antiqua

Visit our website at
www.stonebunnypress.ca

ISBN: 978-0-9947556-5-0

10 9 8 7 6 5 4 3 2 1

Published in Canada

On the Road in the Hundred Years War

Tales from Froissart Volume 1

Translated by Thomas Johnes

Edited by Steven Muhlberger

Other Books by Stonebunny Press

Poetry

Blue City by Dale Percy

Medieval Recreation

The Book of Chivalry of Sir Nigel MacFarlane by Todd H. C. Fischer

A Knight on Vigil by Finnvarr de Taahe

The Dialogue of Chivalry of Duke Finnvarr de Taahe by Finnvarr de Taahe

Folklore

A Canadian Bestiary by Todd H. C. Fischer

Horror

Deadstock by Ian Rogers

Can-Lit

The Other Voice by K. D. Miller

On the Road in the Hundred Years War

Preface – Jean Froissart, researcher and storyteller

Jean Froissart (d.) was a cleric, a poet and a historian whose chief subject was the Hundred Years War, which began in his early youth and continued long after he died. Froissart was very popular with readers in his own lifetime, and has been ever since. This collection of excerpts from his vast *Chronicles* should give you an idea of why his work has been copied, illuminated, printed, and translated many times and why he has been called "the Secretary of Chivalry."

The texts I have used for this series are taken from the translation of Thomas Johnes (1805). With a very few exceptions the spelling, capitalization, and phrasing found here are taken directly from Johnes. Citations by book, chapter, volume and page are those of the 1862 two-volume reprint of Johnes.

Some further commentary can be found at the end of the book. But first, let us ride with Froissart through the south of France and listen while he collects stories from the men who fought the Hundred Years War.

On his way to Foix, Froissart falls in with a knight who knows much about local events.

Book III, ch. 4 (Johnes, v. 2, pp. 60-1). At the time I undertook my journey to visit the count de Foix, reflecting on the diversity of countries I had never seen, I set out from Carcassonne, leaving the road to Toulouse on the right hand, and came to Monteroral, then to Tonges, then to Belle, then to the first town in the county of Foix; from thence to Maisieres, to the castle of Sauredun, then to the handsome city of Pamiers, which belongs to the count de Foix, where I halted, to wait for company that were going to Béarn, where the count resided. I remained in the city of Pamiers three days: it is a very delightful place, seated among fine vineyards, and surrounded by a clear and broad river, called the Liege.

Accidentally, a knight attached to the count de Foix, called sir Espaign du Lyon, came thither, on his return from Avignon: he was a prudent and valiant knight, handsome in person, and about fifty years of age. I introduced myself to his company, as he had a great desire to know what was doing in France. We were six days on the road travelling to Orthès.

As we journeyed, the knight, after saying his orisons, conversed the greater part of the day with me, asking for news; and when I put any questions to him, he very willingly answered them. On our departure from Pamiers we crossed the mountain of Cesse, which is difficult of ascent, and passed near the town and castle of Ortingas, which belongs to the king of France, but did not enter it. We went to dine at a castle of the count de Foix, half a league further, called Carlat, seated on a high mountain.

After dinner, the knight said: "Let us ride gently, we have but two leagues of this country (which are equal to three of

France) to our lodging."

"Willingly," answered I.

"Now," said the knight, "we have this day passed the castle of Ortingas, the garrison of which did great mischief to all this part of the country. Peter d'Anchin had possession of it: he took it by surprise, and has gained sixty thousand francs from France."

"How did he get so much?" said I.

"I will tell you," replied the knight. "On the feast of our lady, the middle of August, a fair is holden, where all the country assemble, and there is much merchandise brought thither during that time. Peter d'Anchin and his companions of the garrison of Lourde, had long wanted to gain this town and castle, but could not devise the means. They had, however, in the beginning of May, sent two of their men, of very simple outward appearance, to seek for service in the town: they soon found masters, who were so well satisfied with them, that they went in and out of the town whenever they pleased, without any one having the smallest suspicion of them.

"When mid-August arrived, the town was filled with foreign merchants from Foix, Béarn, and France: and, you know, when merchants meet, after any considerable absence, they are accustomed to drink plentifully together to renew their acquaintance, so that the houses of the masters of these two servants were quite filled, where they drank largely, and their landlords with them.

"At midnight Peter d'Anchin and his company advanced towards Ortingas, and hid themselves and horses in the wood through which we passed. He sent six varlets with two ladders to the town, who, having crossed the ditches where they had been told was the shallowest place, fixed their ladders against the walls: the two pretended servants, who were in waiting, assisted them (whilst their masters were seated at table) to mount the walls. They were no sooner up, than one of the servants conducted their companions towards the gate where only two men guarded the keys: he then said to them, 'Do you remain here, and not stir until you shall hear me whistle; then sally forth and slay the guards. I am well acquainted with the keys, having more than seven times guarded the gate with my master.'

"As he had planned so did they execute, and hid themselves well. He then advanced to the gate, and, having listened, found the watch drinking: he called to them by their names, for he was well acquainted with them, and said, 'Open the door: I bring you the best wine you ever tasted, which my master sends you that you may watch the better.' Those who knew the varlet imagined he was speaking truth, and opened the door of the guard-room: upon this, he whistled, and his companions sallied forth and pushed between the door, so that they could not shut it again. The guards were thus caught cunningly, amid so quietly slain that no one knew anything of it. They then took the keys and went to the gate, which they opened, and let down the draw-bridge so gently it was not heard. This done, they sounded a horn with one blast only, which those in ambuscade hearing, they mounted their horses and came full gallop over the bridge into the town, where they took all its inhabitants either at table or in their beds. Thus was Ortingas taken by Peter d'Anchin of Bigorre and his companions in Lourde."

I then asked the knight, "But how did they gain the castle?"

"I will tell you," said sir Espaign du Lyon. "At the time the town was taken, by ill-luck the governor was absent, supping with some merchants from Carcassonne, so that he was made prisoner, and on the morrow Peter d'Anchin had him brought before the castle, wherein were his wife and children, whom he frightened by declaring he would order the governor's head to be struck off, if they did not enter into a treaty to deliver up the castle. It was concluded, that if his lady would surrender, the governor should be given up to her, with permission to march unmolested away with everything that belonged to them.

The lady, who found herself in such a critical situation, through love to him who could not now defend her, in order to recover her husband and to avoid greater dangers, surrendered the castle, when the governor, his wife and children, set out with all that belonged to them, and went to Pamiers. By this means, Peter d'Anchin captured the town and castle of Ortingas; and, when they entered the place, he and his companions gained thirty thousand francs, as well in merchandise which they found there as in good French prisoners. All those who were from the county of Foix or Béarn received their liberty, with their goods untouched.

"Peter d'Anchin held Ortingas for full five years; and he and his garrison made frequent excursions as far as the gates of Carcassonne, which is sixteen long leagues distant, greatly ruining the country as well by the ransoms of towns which compounded, as by the pillage they made. During the time Peter d'Anchin garrisoned Ortingas, some of his companions made a sally, being desirous of gain, and came to a castle a good league off, called le Paillier, of which Raymond du Paillier, a French knight, was the lord. They this time accomplished their enterprise, having before attempted it in vain; and, by means of a scalado, they took the castle, the knight and his lady in bed. They kept possession of it, allowing the lady and the children to depart, but detained the knight four months in his own castle, until he had paid four thousand francs for his ransom. In short, after they had sufficiently harassed the country, they sold these two castles, Ortingas and le Paillier, for eight thousand francs, and then retired to Lourde, their principal garrison. Such feats of arms and adventures were these companions daily practising.

"It happened likewise at this time, that a very able man at arms, one of the garrison of Lourde, a Gascon, called le Mengeant de Sainte Basile, set out from Lourde with twenty-nine others, and rode towards the Toulousain and the Albigeois, seeking adventures. His wishes were to surprise the castle of Penne in the Albigeois, which he was nearly doing, but failed. When he found he was disappointed, he rode up to the gate, where he skirmished, and several gallant deeds were done. At this same hour, the castellan of Toulouse, sir Hugh de Froide-ville, had also made an excursion with sixty lances, and by accident arrived at Penne whilst this skirmish was going forward. He and his men instantly dismounted, and advanced to the barriers. Le Mengeant would have made off; but, as that was impossible, he fought valiantly hand to hand with the knight: he behaved gallantly, and wounded his adversary in two or three places, but at last was made prisoner; for he was not the strongest; and of his men few escaped being killed or taken. Le Mengeant was carried to Toulouse; and the seneschal had great difficulty to save him from the populace, who wanted to put him to death when they saw him in the hands of their own officer, so much was he hated at Toulouse.

"Fortunately for him, the duke of Berry chanced to come to that city, and he had such good friends that the duke gave him his liberty in consideration of a thousand francs being paid the seneschal for his ransom. Le Mengeant, on gaining his liberty, returned to Lourde, where he ceased not from his usual enterprises.

"One time he set out with others, without arms, disguised as an abbot attended by four monks; for he and his companions had shaven the crowns of their heads, and no one would have imagined who saw them but that they were real monks, for they had every appearance in dress and look. In this manner he came to Montpelier, and alighted at the hotel of the Angel, saying he was an abbot from Upper Gascony going to Paris on business. He made acquaintance with a rich man of Montpelier, called sir Beranger, who was likewise bound for Paris on his affairs. On the abbot telling him he would carry him thither free from all expense, he was delighted that the journey would cost him nothing, and set out with le Mengeant attended only by a servant. They had not left Montpelier three leagues when le Mengeant made him his prisoner, and conducted him through crooked and bye-roads to his garrison of Lourde, whence he afterwards ransomed him for five thousand francs."

"Holy Mary !" cried I, "this le Mengeant must have been a clever fellow."

"Aye, that he was indeed," replied he; "and he died in his armour at a place we shall pass in three days, called Larre in Bigorre, below a town called Archinach."

"I will remind you of it," said I, "when we shall arrive at the spot."

***

Book III, ch. 5 (Johnes, v. 2, pp. 78-9). Thus rode we on to Montesquieu, a good inclosed town belonging to the count de Foix. which the Armagnacs and Labrissiens took by surprise, but held it only three days; in the morning we left Montesquieu, and rode towards Palaminich, another inclosed town, situated on the Garonne, and belonging to the count de Foix. When we were close to it, and thought of entering it by the bridge over the Garonne, we found it impossible; for the preceding day it had rained so heavily in the mountains of Catalonia and Arragon, that a river, called the Saluz, which rises among them, and falls into the Garonne with great rapidity, was so much swelled as to carry away one of the arches of the bridge, which was of wood. We were therefore forced to return to Montesquieu to dinner, and remain there the whole day.

On the morrow, the knight was advised to cross the Garonne, opposite the town of Casseres, in a boat; we therefore rode thither, and by our exertions the horses passed, and we ourselves afterwards with some difficulty and danger; for the boat was so small that only two horses and their men could cross at a time with those who managed the boat. When we had crossed, we made for Casseres, where we staid the whole day.

While our servants were preparing the supper, sir Espaign du Lyon said, "Sir John, let us go and see the town."

"Come then," replied I. We walked through the town to a gate which opens towards Palaminich, and, having passed it, went near the ditches. The knight, pointing to the walls; said, "Do you observe that part of the walls?"

"Yes, sir: why do you ask?"

"I will tell you: because it is newer than the rest."

"That is true," answered I.

"I will relate to you how this happened ten years ago. You have heard of the wars between the count d'Armagnac and the count de Foix, which took place in the country of Béarn, that appertains to the count de Foix: the count d'Armagnac overran it, though at present he is quiet on account of the truces made between them. I must say, the Armagnacs and Labrissiens gained nothing, but had often great losses. On the night of the feast of St. Nicholas, in the winter of the year 1362, the count de Foix made prisoners, near to Montmarsen, the count d'Armagnac and his nephew the lord d'Albreth, and many nobles with them, whom he carried to Orthès, and confined them in the tower of the castle; by which capture he received ten times told one hundred thousand francs.

"It happened afterwards that the count d'Armagnac, father of the present, called, sir John d'Armagnac, set on foot an armament, with which he came and took Casseres by scalado: they were full two hundred men at arms, who seemed resolved to keep the place by force. News was brought to the count de Foix, at Pan, that the Armagnacs and Labrissiens had taken his town of Casseres. He, who was a prudent and valiant knight, and prepared for all events, called to him two bastard brothers whom he had among his knights, sir Arnault Guillaume and sir Peter de Béarn, and ordered them to march instantly to Casseres, telling them he would send men from all parts, and in three days would be there in person.

" 'Be careful therefore,' added he, 'that none get out of the town without being fought with, as you will have strength enough; and on your arrival at Casseres make the country people bring you plenty of large pieces of wood, which you will fix strongly round the gates, and completely bar them up; for I am resolved that those now in the town shall be so shut up in it, that they never pass through the gates: I will make them take another road.'

"The two knights obeyed his orders, and marched to Palaminich, accompanied and followed by all the men at arms in Béarn. They encamped before the town of Casseres; but those within paid no attention to them, nor observed that they were so completely shut in, they could not pass through the gates. On the third day the count de Foix came with five hundred men at arms, and on his arrival had the town encompassed with fortifications of wood, as well as by his army, that no sally might be made from it in the night.

"In this state, without making any attack, he blockaded them until their provisions began to fail; for though they had wine in plenty, they had nothing to eat, and could not escape by fording the river, which was then too deep. They therefore thought it better to surrender themselves as prisoners, than shamefully perish with hunger. The count de Foix listened to their offers. He had them informed, that as they could not pass through any of the town-gates, he would make a hole in the wall through which the garrison, one by one, must pass, without arms, in their common dress. They were forced to accept of these terms, otherwise the business was at an end: and, if the count de Foix had not been thus appeased, all within were dead men.

"He had a hole made in the wall, which was not too large, through which they came out one by one. The count was there, with his forces drawn up in battle-array; and as they came out of the town they were brought before him, and sent to different castles and towns as prisoners. He took there his cousin, sir John d'Armagnac, sir Bertrand d'Albreth, sir Manaut de Barbasan, sir Raymond de Benach, sir Benedict de la Corneille, and about twenty of the most respectable, whom he carried with him to Orthès, and received from them, before they gained their liberty, one hundred thousand francs, twice told. For this, my fair sir, was this wall broken down; as a passage for those of Armagnac and Albreth: afterwards it was rebuilt and repaired."

When he had finished his history we returned to our lodgings, and found the supper ready.

On the morrow we mounted our horses, and riding up the side of the Garonne, passed through Palaminich, and entered the lands of the counts de Comminges and d'Armagnac. On the opposite side, fronting us, was the Garonne, and the territories of the count de Foix. As we rode on, the knights pointed out to me a town, which appeared tolerably strong, called Marteras le Toussac, which belongs to the count de Comminges; and on the other side of the river, two castles of the count de Foix, seated on a mountain called Montaural and Monclare.

As we were riding among these towns and castles, in a beautiful meadow by the side of the Garonne, the knight said,"Sir John, I have witnessed here many excellent skirmishes and combats between the Armagnacs and the Foixiens; for there was neither town nor castle that was not well garrisoned with men at arms, who engaged with and pursued each other. Do you see yonder those ruins? they are the remains of a fort which the Armagnacs raised against these two castles, and which they filled with men at arms, who did much damage to the lands of the count de Foix, on the other side of the river; but I will tell you how they paid for it. The count de Foix one night sent his brother, sir Peter de Béarn, with two hundred lances and four hundred peasants, laden with faggots, and as much wood as they could cut front the hedges, which they piled around this fort and set on fire, so that the fort was burnt with all in it, for none received quarter; and since that time no one has dared to rebuild it."

***

Sir Espaign du Lyon continues to tell stories to Froissart as they travel to Foix.

Joute de Vannes (1381 ap. J.-C.) dans les Chroniques de Jean Froissart - XIV -XVe siècle
BNF RC-A-66392 FRANCAIS 2676 v

Book III, ch. 5 (Johnes, v. 2, pp. 79-80). ...With such conversation did we daily travel, travelling towards the source of the river Garonne, on each side of which were handsome castles and forts. All on the left hand belonged to the count de Foix, and on the other to the count d'Armagnac. We passed Montpesac, a fine strong castle, seated on the top of a rock, below which is the road and the town. On the outside of it, at the distance of a cross-bow, there is a pass called la Garde, with a tower between the rock and the river, and an iron gate: six men could defend this pass against all the world, for only two persons abreast can advance between the rock and river.

Upon seeing this, I said to the knight, "Sir, this is a strong pass, and a difficult country."

"It is, indeed," answered the knight; "but, strong as it is, the count de Foix and. his men once forced it, and advanced to Palaminich, Montesquieu, and even to Pamiers. The pass was very strong, but the English archers greatly assisted him in this conquest. Come and ride by my side, and I will tell you all about it." I then rode by the side of sir Espaign du Lyon, who thus continued his narration: "The count d'Armagnac and the lord d'Albreth invaded the country of Foix, with upwards of five hundred men, and advanced into those parts near Pamiers. It was in the beginning of August, when the corn was harvesting and the grapes ripe: in that year there was great abundance of both. Sir John d'Armagnac and his people were encamped before the town and castle of Sauredun, a short league distant from Pamiers. They made an attack on it, and sent word to Pamiers, that if they did not pay a composition for their corn and wines, they would burn and destroy all.

Those of Pamiers were afraid of waiting the event, as their lord was at too great a distance, being then in Béarn, so that they thought it more prudent to pay the ransom, which was settled at five thousand francs; but they demanded a delay of fifteen days, which was granted to them.

The count de Foix heard of all this, and, by great haste and sending to all parts for aid, he got into Pamiers through this difficult pass. Assistance came to him from several quarters, so that he found himself at the head of twelve hundred lances: he would have given battle, without fail, to sir John d'Armagnac, if he had waited for it; but they retreated into the country of Comminges, leaving behind the money from Pamiers, as they had no time to stay for it.

The count de Foix, however, did not hold them quit, but claimed the ransom, as he said he had deserved it; for he had come to their assistance, and to drive his enemies out of the country. He paid with it his men at arms, and remained there until the good people had harvested their corn, finished their vintage, and put all their effects in safety."

"By my faith," said I to the knight, "I have heard you with pleasure."

Thus discoursing, we passed near a castle called la Bretite, and then another castle called Bacelles, all in the county of Comminges.

As I rode on, I saw on the other side of the river a very handsome and large castle, with a town of goodly appearance. I asked the knight the name of this castle. He told me it was called Montesplain, and belonged to a cousin of the count de Foix, who bears the cows in his arms, named sir Roger d'Espaign. He is a great baron and hand proprietor in this country and in the Toulousain, and at this moment is seneschal of Carcassone.

Upon which I asked, "What relation was this sir Roger d'Espaign to sir Charles d'Espaign, constable of France."

"He is not of that family," replied the knight; "for sir Lewis and sir Charles d'Espaign, of whom you are speaking, came originally from Spain, and were of Spanish extraction; but by their mothers are of French also, and cousins-german to king Alfonso of Spain. I served in my youth under sir Lewis d'Espaign, in the wars of Brittany: for he was always of the side of St. Charles de Blois against the count de Montfort." Here ended our conversation on this subject.

We came that day to St. Gouffors, a good town belonging to the count de Foix, and on the morrow to dinner at Moncuil, a strong town also, which belongs to the king of France and is held by sir Roger d'Espaign. After dinner, we mounted and took the road towards Lourde and Malvoisin, and rode over heaths that extend fifteen leagues: they are called Lane-bourg, and are well calculated for those who are evil-inclined. Amid the heaths of Lane-bourg is situated the castle de la Mesere, belonging to the count de Foix, a good league above the town of Tournay and below Malvoisin, which castle the knight showed me, saying,-"See, yonder is Malvoisin: have you not inserted in your history (of which you have been speaking to me) how the duke of Anjou, when he was in this country, advanced to Lourde, besieged and conquered it, as well as the castle of Trigalet on the river before us, and which belongs to the lord de la Barde?"

I considered a little, and replied; "I believe I have not mentioned it, nor have I ever been informed of such an event. I therefore pray you relate the business, to which I shall attentively listen; but tell me, lest I forget it, what is become of the river Garonne? for I can no longer see it."

"You say truly," answered the knight: "it loses itself between these two mountains. It rises from a spring three leagues off, on the road to Catalonia, below a castle called St. Béart, the last castle of France on the frontiers of Arragon. The governor of it and the surrounding country at this time is a squire named Ernauton, who is called the Bastard of Spain, and cousin-german to sir Roger d'Espaign. The moment you see him you will say, he is formed for a downright man at arms. This bastard of Spain has done more mischief to the garrison of Lourde than all the knights and squires of this country together; and I must say, the count de Foix loves him well, for he is his brother in arms. I will not say more of him, for, at the ensuing Christmas, you will see him yourself at the hotel of the count; but I will tell you what the duke of Anjou did when he was in this country."

***

Sir Espaign du Lyon tells more stories to Froissart as they travel to Foix.

Book III, ch. 6 (Johnes, v. 2, pp. 81-4). We then rode gently, and he began his narration as follows: "At the first renewal of the war, the French conquered back again from the English all their possessions in Aquitaine, and sir Oliver de Clisson, having turned to the French interest, conducted the duke of Anjou as you know, into Brittany to the estates of sir Robert Knolles and to the siege of Derval; all which, I dare say, you have in your history, as well as the treaty made by sir Hugh Broc, cousin to sir Robert, to surrender the castle, for which he had given hostages, imagining the duke of Anjou to be in such strength that the siege could not be raised; and you probably relate how sir Robert Knolles, having entered the castle of Derval, refused to abide by this treaty."

"Truly, sir, I have heard all you have just related."

"And have you noticed the skirmish which took place before the castle, when sir Oliver de Clisson was wounded?"

"I cannot say" replied I, "that I have any remembrance of it. Tell me, then, what passed at this skirmish and at the siege; perhaps you may know more particulars than I do; and you can return afterwards to the history of Lourde and Malvoisin."

"That is true," said the knight: "I must tell you, however, that sir Garsis du Chatel, a very valiant knight of this country and a good Frenchman, had gone to seek the duke, to conduct him before Malvoisin, when the duke had issued his summons to march to Derval: He made sir Garsis marshal of his army for his valour.

It is a truth, as I was informed afterwards, that when sir Garsis found sir Robert determined not to keep the treaty, and the castle of Derval not likely to surrender, he came to the duke and asked, 'My lord, what shall we do with these hostages? It is no fault nor crime in them if the castle be not surrendered; and it will be a great sin if you put them to deaths, for they are gentlemen undeserving such punishment.'

"The duke replied, 'Is it right, then, that they should have their liberty?'

" 'Yes, by my faith,' said the knight, who had such compassion for them.

" 'Go,' replied the duke,' and do with them what you please.'

"At these words, as sir Garsis told me, he went to deliver them, but in his road met sir Oliver de Clisson, who asked him whence he came, and whither he was going. 'I come from my lord of Anjou, and am going to set at liberty the hostages.'

" 'To set them at liberty?' said sir Oliver: stop a little, and come with me to the duke.' On his return, he found the duke very pensive. Sir Oliver saluted him, and then said, ' My lord, what are your intentions? shall not these hostages be put to death ? By my faith shall they, in spite of sir Robert Knolles and sir Hugh Broc, who have belied their faith: and I would have you know, if they do not suffer deaths, I will not, for a year to come, put on a helmet to serve you; they will come off too cheaply, if they be thus acquitted. This siege has cost you sixty thousand francs, and you wish to pardon your enemies who keep no faith with you.'

"At these words, the duke of Anjou grew wroth, and said, 'Sir Oliver, do with them as you wish.'

" 'I will, them, that they die; for there is cause for it, since they keep not their faiths.' He then left the duke and went to his square before the castle; but sir Garsis never dared to say one word in their favour, for it would have been lost labour, since sir Oliver was determined upon it. He called to him Jocelin, who was the headsman, and ordered him to behead two knights and two squires, which caused such grief that upwards of two hundred of the army wept.

"Sir Robert Knolles instantly opened a postern-gate of the castle, and had, in revenge, all his prisoners beheaded, without sparing one. The great gate was then opened, and the drawbridge let down, when the garrison made a sally beyond the barriers to skirmish with the French, which, according to sir Garsis, was a severe business: the first arrow wounded sir Oliver de Clisson, who retired to his quarters. Among the wounded were two squires from Béarn, who behaved themselves well: their names were Bertrand de Barege and Ernauton du Pin.

"On the morrow they decamped. The duke marched with his

men at arms from Derval to Toulouse, and from thence to this country, with intent to destroy Lourde, for the Toulousains made great complaints of it. What happened there I will tell you. The duke lost no time in marching his army to the castle of Malvoisin, which we see before us, and laying siege to it. He had in his army full eight thousand combatants, without reckoning the Genoese and the commonalty from the principal towns in that country.

"A Gascon squire and able man at arms, named Raymonet de l'Epée, was at that time governor of Malvoisin. There were daily skirmishes at the barriers, where many gallant feats were done by those who wished to advance themselves. The duke and his army were encamped in these handsome meadows between the town of Tournay and the castle, on the banks of the Lisse.

"During this siege, sir Garsis du Châtel, who was marshal of the army, marched with five hundred men at arms, two hundred archers and cross-bows, and full two thousand common men, to lay siege to the castle of Trigalet, which we have left behind us. A squire of Gascony had the command of it, for his cousin the lord de la Barde, and was called the Bascot de Mauléon: he had about forty companions with him, who were lords of Lane-bourg; for no one could march through these parts except a pilgrim to the shrine of St. Jago, without being made a prisoner, and, if not ransomed, put to death. There was another strong place, near to le Mesen, of which thieves and robbers from all countries made a garrison, called le Nemilleux: it is very strong, but always in dispute between the count d'Armagnac and the count de Foix; and for this reason the nobles paid not any attention to it when the duke of Anjou came into the country.

"Sir Garsis, on arriving at Trigalet, had it surrounded on all sides but that towards the river, which they could not approach, and a sharp attack commenced, in which many of each party were wounded. Sir Garsis was five days there, and on every one of them were skirmishes; insomuch that the garrison had expended all their ammunition, and had nothing left to shoot with, which was soon perceived by the French. Upon this, sir Garsis, out of true gallantry, sent a passport to the governor to come and speak with him. When he saw him, he said, 'Bascot, I well know your situation; that your garrison have no ammunition, nor anything but lances to defend themselves with when attacked. Now, if you be taken by storm, it will be impossible for me to save yours or your companions' lives, from the fury of the common people, for which I should be very sorry, as you are my cousin. I therefore advise you to surrender the place, and even entreat you so to do: you cannot be blamed by any one for it, and seeking fortune elsewhere, for you have held out long enough.'

"'My lord,' replied the squire, 'anywhere but here I would freely do what you advise, for in truth I am your cousin: in this instance, I cannot act from myself, for those who are with me have an equal command, though they affect to consider me as their captain. I will return, and tell them what you have said: if they agree to surrender, I shall consent; if they be resolved to hold out, whatever may be my fate, I must, with them, abide the event.'

"'This is well said,' answered sir Garsis: 'you may depart whenever you please, since I know your intention.'

"The Bascot de Mauléon returned to the castle, and assembled all his companions in the court-yard, to whom he related what sir Garsis had said, and then demanded their opinions, and what they would do. They debated for a long time: some said they were strong enough to wait the event: others wished to withdraw, saying it was full time for it, as they had no longer any ammunition, and the duke of Anjou was severe, and the whole country of Toulouse and Carcassone enraged against them for the mischiefs they had done.

"Everything having been considered, they agreed to surrender the castle, but on condition they should be escorted, themselves and baggage, to chateau Cullie, which their friends were in possession of, on the Toulousain frontier. Upon this, Bascot de Mauléon returned to sir Garsis who granted their demand; for he saw the castle was not easy to win by storm, and it would probably have cost him many lives. They made their preparations to depart, packing up everything they could. Of pillage they had enough, and carried away the best part of it, leaving the rest behind them. Sir Garsis had them safely escorted as far as chateau Cullie. By this means did the French gain the castle of Trigalet, which sir Garsis gave to the commonalty of the country who had accompanied him, to do with it what they chose. They determined to destroy and raze it, in the manner you have seen, which was so completely done, that no one since has ever thought of rebuilding it.

"Sir Garsis would have marched from thence to castle Nautilleux, which is situated on the moors near the castle of Lamen, to free it from those companions who had possession of it; but on the road they told him" "My lord, you have no need to advance further, for you will not find any one in castle Nautilleux : those who were there are fled, some one way, some another, we know not whither.'

"Sir Garsis, on hearing this, halted in the plain to consider what was best to be done. The seneschal de Nobesen happened to be present, who said, 'Sir, this castle is within my jurisdiction, and should be held from the count de Foix give it me, I beg of you, and I will have it so well guarded at my costs, that no person who wishes ill to the country shall ever enter it.'

*Bataille de Poitiers (1356), l'arrestation du roi Jean le Bon Besançon,
bibliothèque municipal*

*Illustration extraite des Chroniques de Jean Froissart,
ms 864, fol. 172*

"'My lord,' added those from Toulouse who were by, 'he speaks well: the seneschal is a valiant and prudent man, and it is better he should have it than another.'

"'I consent to it,' said sir Garsis. Thus was the castle of Nantilleux given to the seneschal de Nobesen, who rode thither, and, having found it empty, had repaired what had been destroyed. He appointed governor a squire of the country named Fortifie de St. Pol, and then returned to the siege of Malvoisin where the duke was. Sir Garsis and his men had already related to the duke their successful exploits.

"The castle of Malvoisin held out about six weeks; there were, daily, skirmishes between the two armies at the barriers, and the place would have made a longer resistance, for the castle was so strong it could have held a long siege; but, the well that supplied the castle with water being without the walls, they cut off the communication: the weather was very hot, and the cisterns within quite dry, for it had not rained one drop for six weeks; and the besiegers were at their ease on the banks of this clear and fine river, which they made use of for themselves and horses.

"The garrisons of Malvoisin were alarmed at their situation, for they could not hold out longer: they had a sufficiency of wine, but not one drop of sweet water. They determined to open a treaty; and Raymonet de l'Epée requested a passport to wait on the duke, which having easily obtained, he said, 'My lord, if you will act courteously to me and my companions, I will surrender the castle of Malvoisin.'

"'What courtesy is it you ask?' replied the duke of Anjou: 'get about your business, each of you to your own countries, without entering any fort that holds out against us; for if you do so, and I get hold of you, I will deliver you up to Jocelin, who will shave you without a razor.'

"'My lord,' answered Raymonet, if we thus depart, we must carry away what belongs to us, and what we have gained by arms and with great risks.'

"The duke paused a while, and then said, 'I consent that you take with you whatever you can carry before you in trunks and on sumpter-horses, but not otherwise; and, if you have any prisoners, they must be given up to us.'

"'I agree,' said Raymonet. Such was the treaty, as you hear me relate it; and all who were in the castle departed, after surrendering it to the duke of Anjou and carrying all they could with them. They returned to their own country, or elsewhere, in search of adventures: but Raymonet l'Epée turned to the French: he served the duke of Anjou a long time, passed into Italy with him, and was killed in a skirmish before the city of Naples.

"Thus, my fair sir, did the duke of Anjou at that time conduct himself, and win the castle of Malvoisin, which gave him great joy. He made governor of it a knight of Bigorre, called sir Ciquart de Luperiere, and afterwards gave it to the count de Foix, who still holds it, and will do so as long as he lives; for it is well guarded by a knight of Bigorre, a relation of his, called sir Raymond de Lane.

"The duke of Anjou having gained possession of Malvoisin, and freed the country, and all Lane-bourg, of the English and other pillagers, laid siege to the town and castle of Lourde. The count de Foix, seeing him so near his territories, began to be very doubtful what his intentions might be. He therefore issued his summons to his knights and squires, and sent them into different garrisons. He placed his brother, sir Arnaut William, with two hundred lances, in Morlens; his other brother, sir Peter de Béarn, with the same number of lances, in Pan; sir Peter de Cabesten, with the like number, in the city of l'Estrade; sir Mouvant de Novalles in the town of Hertillet, with one hundred lances; sir Crual Geberel in Montgerbiel with the like number; sir Fouquat d'Orterey in the town of Sauveterre with the same; and I, Espaign du Lyon, was sent to Mont-de-marsen with two hundred lances. There was not a castle in all Béarn that was not well provided with men at arms: he himself remained to guard his florins in the castle of Orthès."

***

Sir Espaign du Lyon has been telling Froissart how the count of Foix had men-at-arms in every castle in Béarn.

Book III, ch. 6 (Johnes, v. 2, pp. 84). "The duke of Anjou having gained possession of Malvoisin, and freed the country, and all Lane-bourg, of the English and other pillagers, laid siege to the town and castle of Lourde. The count de Foix, seeing him so near his territories, began to be very doubtful what his intentions might be. He therefore issued his summons to his knights and squires, and sent them into different garrisons. He placed his brother, sir Arnaut William, with two hundred lances, in Morlens; his other brother, sir Peter de Béarn, with the same number of lances, in Pan; sir Peter de Cabesten, with the like number, in the city of l'Estrade; sir Mouvant de Novalles in the town of Hertillet, with one hundred lances; sir Crual Geberel in Montgerbiel with the like number; sir Fouquat d'Orterey in the town of Sauveterre with the same; and I, Espaign du Lyon, was sent to Mont-de-marsen with two hundred lances. There was not a castle in all Béarn that was not well provided with men at arms: he himself remained to guard his florins in the castle of Orthès."

"Sir," said I to the knight, "has he a great quantity of them?"

"By my faith," replied he, "the count de Foix has at this moment a hundred thousand thirty times told; and there is not a year but he gives away sixty thousand; for a more liberal lord, in making presents, does not exist."

Upon this I asked, "To whom does he make these gifts?" He answered, "To strangers, to knights and squires who travel through his country, to heralds, minstrels, to all who converse with him: none leave him without a present, for he would be angered should any one refuse it."

"Ha, ha, holy Mary! " cried I, "to what purpose does he keep so large a sum? where does it come from? Are his revenues so great to supply him with it? I should like to know this, if you please."

"Yes, you shall know it," answered the knight, "but you have asked two questions: if you wish them answered, I must begin with the first. You ask, for what purpose he keeps so large a sum of money: I must tell you, that the count de Foix is doubtful of war between him and the count d'Armagnac, and of the manoevres of his neighbours the kings of France and of England, neither of whom he would willingly anger; and hitherto he has not taken any part in their wars, for he has never borne arms on either side, and is on good terms with both.

"I tell you, (and you yourself will agree with me when you have made acquaintance with him, and have conversed together, and seen the establishments of his household,) that he is the most prudent prince living, and one whom neither the king of France nor king of England would willingly make an enemy. With regard to his other neighbours, the kings of Arragon and Navarre, he thinks but little of them, for he could instantly raise more men at arms (so many friends has he made by his gifts, and such power has his money,) than these kings could ever do. I have heard him say, that when the King of Cyprus was in Béarn and explained to him the intended expedition to the holy sepulchre, he was so anxious to make that valuable conquest, that if the kings of France and England had gone thither, he would have been the most considerable lord after them, and have led the largest army. He has not yet given up this idea, and it is for this reason also he has amassed such wealth.

"The prince of Wales, likewise, when he reigned in Aquitaine, and resided at Bordeaux, induced him to collect large sums; for the prince menaced him in regard to his country of Béarn, and said he would force him to hold it from him: but the count de Foix declared he would not, for Béarn was free land, and owed no homage to any lord whatever. The prince, who was then very powerful and much feared, said he would make him humble himself; for the count d'Armagnac and the lord d'Ahbreth, who hated the count de Foix for the victories he had gained over them, poisoned the prince's mind. The expedition of the prince into Spain prevented hostilities; and sir John Chandos, who was the principal adviser and much beloved by the prince, strenuously opposed this intended war. The count de Foix and sir John Chandos loved each other for their gallant deeds.

"The count, however, was suspicious of the prince, whom he knew to be powerful and warlike, and began to amass large sums to aid and defend himself should he be attacked. He imposed heavy taxes on the country and on all the towns, which now exist, and will do so as long as he lives: each hearth pays two francs per annum, one with the other; and in this he has found and finds a mine of wealth, for it is marvellous how cheerfully his subjects pay it. With this, there is not any Englishman, Frenchman, nor pillager, who rob his people of a single farthing: his whole country is protected and justice well administered, for in matters of justice he is the most severe and upright lord that exists."

With these words we found ourselves in the town of Tournay, where our lodgings were prepared: the knight, therefore, ceased speaking; and I made no further enquiries, for I had well remarked where he had left off, and could again remind him of it, as we had yet to travel together. We were comfortably lodged at the hotel of the Star. When supper was served, the governor of Malvoisin, sir Raymond de Lane, came to see us, and supped with us: he brought with him four flagons of excellent wine, as good as any I drank on the road. These two knights conversed long together, and it was late when sir Raymond departed and returned to his castle of Malvoisin.

***

Sir Espaign du Lyon continues to entertain Froissart as they travel to Foix.

Book III, ch. 7 (Johnes, v. 2, pp. 85-7). In the morning, we mounted our horses, set out from Tournay, passed the river Lisse at a ford; and, riding towards the city of Tarbes, entered Bigorre, leaving on our left the road to Lourde, Bagneres and the castle of Montgaillard. We made for a village called in the country Terra Cimitat, and skirted a wood, which we afterwards entered, on the lands of the lord de Barbasan; when the knight said, "Sir John, this is the pass of Larre: look about you. I did so, and thought it a very strange country, and should have imagined myself in great danger if I had not had the company of the knight."

I recollected what he had said some days before respecting the country of Larre and Mengeant de Lourde, and, reminding him of them, said, "My lord, you promised that when we came to the country of Larre, you would tell me more of Mengeant de Lourde, and the manner of his death."

"It is true," replied the knight: come and ride by my side, and I will tell it you." I then pushed forward to hear him the better, when he began as follows:

"During the time Peter d'Anchin held the castle and garrison of Ortingas, as I have before related, those of Lourde made frequent excursions at a distance from their fort, when they had not always the advantage. You see those two castles of Barbasan and Marteras, which had always considerable garrisons: the towns of Bagneres, Tournay, Montgaillard, Salenges, Benach, Gorre, and Tarbes, were also full of French troops. When they heard that those of Lourde had made any excursion towards Toulouse or Carcassone, they collected themselves and formed an ambuscade, to slay them and carry off what pillage they should have collected: sometimes several on each side were killed, at others those of Lourde passed unmolested.

"It happened once, that Ernauton de Sainte Colombe, le Mengeant de Sainte Corneille, with six score lances, good men at arms, set out from Lourde, and advanced round the mountains between the two rivers Lisse and Lesse, as far as Toulouse. On their return, they found in the meadows great quantities of cattle, pigs, and sheep, which they seized, as well as some substantial men from the flat countries, and drove them all before them.

"It was told to the governor of Tarbes, a squire of Gascony, called Ernauton Biffete, how those of Lourde were overrunning and harassing the country, and he sent information of this to the lord de Benach and to Enguerros de

Lane, son of sir Raymond, and also to the lord de Barbasan, adding, he was determined to attack them. These knights and squires of Bigorre, having agreed to join him, assembled their men in the town of Tournay, through which the garrison of Lourde generally returned. The bourg d'Espaign had come thither from his garrison of St. Béart, and they were in the whole two hundred lances. They had sent spies into the country to see what appearance their enemies made on their return.

"On the other hand, those from Lourde had likewise spies on the watch, to observe if there were any men at arms out to intercept them: both parties were so active, that each knew the force of the other. When those of Lourde heard that the French garrisons were waiting for them at Tournay, they began to be alarmed, and called a council to determine how to conduct their pillage in safety. It was resolved to divide themselves into two parties: one, consisting of servants and pillagers, was to drive the booty, and take bye roads to Lane-bourg crossing the bridge of Tournay, and the river Lesse between Tournay and Malvoisin: the other division was to march in order of battle on the high grounds, and to make an appearance as if they meant to return by the pass of Larre below Marteras, but to fall back between Barbasan and Montgaillard, in order that the baggage might cross the river in safety. They were to meet all together at Montgaillard, from whence they would soon be at Lourde.

"This plan they executed: and the bastard de Carnillac, Guillonet de Harnes, Perot Boursier, John Calemin de Basselle, and le Rouge Ecuyer, collected forty lances, with all the servants and pillagers, and. said to them, 'You will conduct our plunder and prisoners by the road to Lane-bourg, and then descend between Tournay and Malvoisin, where you will cross the river at the bridge: follow then the bye road between Cimitat and Montgaillard: we will go the other road by

Marteras and Barbasan, so as to meet all together at Montgaillard.' On this they departed; and there remained with the principal division Ernauton de Resten, Ernauton de Sainte Colombe, le Mengeant de Sainte Corneille, and full eighty companions, all men at arms: there were not ten varlets among them. They tightened their armour, fixed their helmets, and, grasping their lances, marched in close order as if they were instantly to engage: they indeed expected nothing else, for they knew their enemies were in the field.

"The French, in like manner as those of Lourde, had called a council respecting their mode of acting. Sir Monant de Barbasan and Ernauton Biscete said: 'Since we know the men of Lourde are bringing home great plunder and many prisoners, we shall be much vexed if they escape us: let us, therefore, form two ambuscades, for we are enow for both.' Upon this it was ordered, that the bourg d'Espaign, sir Raymond de Benach, and Enguerros de Lane, with one hundred spears, should guard the passage at Tournay, for the cattle and prisoners must necessarily cross the river; and the lord de Barbasan and Ernauton Biscete, with the other hundred lances, should reconnoitre, if perchance they could come up with them. They separated from each other, and the lord de Benach, and the bourg d'Espaign, placed themselves in ambuscade at the bridge between Tournay and Malvoisin. The other division rode to the spot where we now are, which is called the Larre, and there the two parties met. They instantly dismounted, and leaving their horses to pasture, with pointed lances advanced, for a combat was unavoidable, shouting their cries, 'St. George for Lourde!' 'Our lady for Bigorre!'

"They charged each other, thrusting their spears with all their strengths, and, to add greater force, urged them forward with their breasts.. The combat was very equal; and for some time none were struck down, as I heard from those present. When

Mahdia-Crusade 1390: The French army disembarking in Africa, led by the duke of Bourbon (Louis II) holding a shield bearing the royal arms of France. (British Library, Royal 14 D VI f. 84v)

http://www.bl.uk/catalogues/illuminatedmanuscripts/ILLUMIN.AS P?Size=mid&IllID=2170

they had sufficiently used their spears, they threw them down, and with battle-axes began to deal out terrible blows on both sides. This action lasted for three hours, and it was marvellous to see how well they fought and defended themselves. When any were so worsted or out of breath, that they could not longer support the fight, they seated themselves near a large ditch full of water in the middle of the plain, when having taken off their helmets, they refreshed themselves: this done, they replaced their helmets and returned to the combat. I do not believe there ever was so well fought or so severe a battle, as this of Marteras in Bigorre, since the famous combat of thirty English against thirty French knights in Brittany .

"They fought hand to hand, and Ernauton de Sainte Colombe, an excellent man at arms, was on the point of being killed by a squire of the country called Guillonet de Salenges, who had pushed him so hard that he was quite out of breath, when I will tell you what happened: Ernauton de Sainte Colombe had a servant who was a spectator of the battle, neither attacking nor attacked by any one; but, seeing his master thus distressed, he ran to him, and, wresting the battle-axe from his hands, said, 'Ernauton, go and sit down: recover yourself: you cannot longer continue the battle.' With this battle-axe he advanced upon the squire, and gave him such a blow on the helmet as made him stagger and almost fall down. Guillonet, smarting from the blow, was very wroth, and made for the servant to strike him with his axe on the head; but the varlet avoided it, and grappling with the squire, who was much fatigued, turned him round, and flung him to the ground under him, when he said, 'I will put you to death, if you do not surrender yourself to my master.'

"'And who is thy master?'

"' Ernauton de Sainte Colombe, with whom you have been so

long engaged.' The squire, finding he had not the advantage, being under the servant, who had his dagger ready to strike, surrendered on condition to deliver himself prisoner within fifteen days, at the castle of Lourde, whether rescued or not.

Of such service was this servant to his master; and, I must say, sir John, that there was a superabundance of feats of arms that day performed, and many companions were sworn to surrender themselves at Tarbes and at Lourde. Ernauton Biscete and le Mengeant de Sainte Basile fought hand to hand, without sparing themselves, and performed many gallant deeds, while all the others were fully employed: however, they fought so vigorously that they exhausted their strength, and both were slain on the spot. Thus fell Ernauton Biscete and le Mengeant de Sainte Basile.

"Upon this, the combat ceased by mutual consent, for they were so worn down that they could not longer wield their axes: some disarmed themselves, to recruit their strength, and left there their arms. Those of Lourde carried with them the dead body of le Mengeant, as the French did that of Ernauton to Tarbes; and, in order that the memory of this battle should be preserved, they erected a cross of stone on the place where these two knights had fought and died. See, there it is: I point to it."

On this, we turned to the right, and made for the cross, when each said an Ave Maria and a Pater-noster for the souls of the deceased.

"By my faith," said I to the knight, " I have listened to you with pleasure; and in truth it was a very severe affair for so small a number; but what became of these who conducted the pillage?"

"I will tell you," replied he. "At the bridge of Tournay, below

Malvoisin, where they intended to cross, they found the bourg d'Espaign in ambuscade, who, on their arrival, sallied out upon them, being in sufficient force. Those of Lourde could not retreat, and were obliged to abide the event. I must truly say, that the combat was as severe and as long, if not longer than that at Marteras. The bourg d'Espaign performed wonders: he wielded a battle-axe, and never hit a man with it but he struck him to the ground. He was well formed for this, being of a large size, strongly made, and not too much loaded with flesh. He took with his own hand the two captains, the bourg de Cornillac and Perot Palatin de Béarn. A squire of Navarre was there slain, called Ferdinand de Miranda, an expert man at arms. Some who were present say the bourg d'Espaign killed him, others that he was stifled through the heat of his armour. In short, the pillage was rescued, and all who conducted it slain or made prisoners; for not three escaped excepting varlets, who ran away and crossed the river Lesse by swimming.

Thus ended this business, and the garrison of Lourde never had such a loss as it suffered that day. The prisoners were courteously ransomed, or mutually exchanged; for those who had been engaged in this combat had made several prisoners on each side, so that it behoved them to treat each other handsomely."

***

Sir Espaign du Lyon tells Froissart another story of the impressive man-at-arms, Ernauton d'Espaign.

Book III, ch. 7 (Johnes, v. 2, p. 87). "Holy Mary !" said I to the knight, "this bourg d'Espaign, is he so strong a man as you tell me?"

"Yes, that he is, by my troth," said he, " and you will not find his equal in all Gascony for vigour of body: it is for thus the count de Foix esteems him as his brother in arms.

"Three years ago, I saw him play a ridiculous trick, which I will relate to you. On Christmas-day, when the count de Foix was celebrating the feast with numbers of knights and squires, as is customary, the weather was piercing cold, and the count had dined, with many lords, in the hall. After dinner he rose and went into a gallery, which has a large staircase of twenty-four steps: in this gallery is a chimney where there is a fire kept when the count inhabits it, otherwise not; and the fire is never great, for he does not like it: it is not for want of blocks of wood, for Béarn is covered with wood in plenty to warm him if he had chosen it, but he has accustomed himself to a small fire.

"When in the gallery he thought the fire too small, for it was freezing and the weather very sharp; and said to the knights around him, 'Here is but a small fire for this weather.' Ernauton d'Espaign instantly ran down stairs; for from the windows of the gallery, which looked into the court, he had seen a number of asses laden with billets of wood for the use of the house, and seizing the largest of these asses, with his load, threw him over his shoulders, and carried him up stairs, pushing through the crowd of knights and squires who were around the chimney, and flung ass and load, with his feet upwards, on the dogs of the hearth, to the delight of the count, and the astonishment of all, at the strength of the squire, who had carried, with such ease, so great a load up so many steps."

This feat of strength did I hear; and all the histories of sir Espaign du Lyon gave me such satisfaction and delight, I thought the road was much too short.

***

Froissart asks his travelling companion, Sir Espaign du Lyon, to tell him more about the campaign of the duke of Anjou against Lourde.

Book III, ch. 7 (Johnes, v. 2, p. 87-90). While this was relating, we crossed the pass of Larre, and leaving the castle of Marteras, where the battle was fought, passed very near the castle of Barbasan, which is handsome and strong, a league distant from Tarbes. We saw it before us, and had a good road, easy to be travelled, following the course of the river Leschez, which rises in the mountains. We rode at our leisure, not to fatigue our horses; and he pointed out to me, on the other side of the river, the castle and town of Montgaillard, and the road which goes straight to Lourde. It then came into my mind to ask the knight about the duke of Anjou, when the castle of Malvoisin had surrendered to him, and how he had acted on his march to Lourde. He very cheerfully told me as follows:

"When the duke of Anjon marched his army from before Malvoisin, he crossed the river Leschez by the bridge of Tournay, and lodged at Bagnères, (where there is a handsome river which runs by Tarbes: for that of Tournay takes a different course, and falls into the Garonne, below Moutmillion) in his way to lay siege to Lourde. Sir Peter Arnaut de Béarn, with his brother John, Peter d'Anchin, Ernauton de Restin, Ernauton de Sainte Colombe, and le Meugeant, who was then alive, Ferdinand de Miranda, Oliver Barhe, le bourg de Cornillac, le bourg Camus, and the other companions within Lourde, had good information of his arrival, and had much strengthened the place, in all respects, against his coming. Lourde held out, in spite of all the attacks they could make on it, for sixteen days consecutively. Many gallant deeds were done, and much mischief to the town by the machines which the duke brought to bear against it, so that at length it was conquered; but the garrison suffered nothing, nor lost man, woman, nor child, for they had all retreated to the castle, as they knew well the town could not always hold out, being only fortified with palisadoes.

"When the French had won the town of Lourde they were much pleased, and, having fixed their quarters in it, they surrounded the castle, which was impregnable but by a long siege. The duke was there upwards of six weeks, and lost more than he gained; for the besiegers could not hurt those within the castle, as it is situated on a perpendicular rock, and can only be approached by ladders, or by one pass. There were at the barriers several handsome skirmishes and deeds of arms, when many squires of France were killed and wounded from having advanced too near. The duke of Anjou, seeing he could not gain the castle of Lourde by force, opened a negociation with the governor, offering him large sums of money if he would surrender his garrison.

The knight was a man of honour, and excused himself by saying, 'the garrison was not his; and that he could neither sell, give, nor alienate the inheritance of the king of England, unless he were a traitor, which he scorned to be, and would remain loyal to his natural lord. When the fort was intrusted to him, it was on condition that he swore solemnly on his faith, in the hands of the prince of Wales, to guard and defend the castle of Lourde until death, against every man whatever, unless he were sent to him from the king of England.' No other answer could be had from him, in reply to all the offers and promises they made; so that, when the duke and his council saw they could not gain anything, they broke up the siege of the castle of Lourde; but, on their decamping, they burnt the town to the ground.

"The duke retreated with his army along the frontiers of Béarn towards Montmarsen: he had heard that the count de Foix had reinforced all his garrisons with men at arms. This did not displease him so much as that the Béarn men should bold out Lourde against him; but he could never obtain anything satisfactory on this head.

"The count de Foix, as I have mentioned before, was very suspicious of the intentions of the duke, who did him no harm, though the count d'Armagnac and the lord d'Albreth wished him to act otherwise; but he was not so inclined. While he was encamped between Montmarsen and the high lands ot Albreth, he sent sir Peter de Benil to Orthès, where on his arrival he was handsomely received by the count de Foix and lodged in the castle. He entertained him splendidly, and presented him with fine horses and mules, and to his people gave other gifts: he sent by him to the duke of Anjou four beautiful horses and two Spanish greyhounds, so handsome and good there were none like them. Some secret negotiations passed between the count and sir Peter de Beuil, of which we knew nothing for a long time; but, from circumstances which shortly happened, we suspected what I will now tell you, and by that time we shall arrive at Tarbes.

"Soon after the duke of Anjou had ended his expedition and was returned to Toulouse, the count de Foix sent letters by a trusty messenger to his cousin sir Peter Arnaut de Béarn at Lourde, for him to come to Orthès. The knight on receiving these letters and noticing the bearer, who was a man of high rank, became very thoughtful and doubtful whether to go or not: however, on full consideration, he said he would go, for he was unwilling to offend the count de Foix.

"When on the point of departure, he called his brother, John de Béarn, and said to him, in presence of the garrison: 'My lord, the count de Foix has sent for me; on what account I know not, but since he is desirous I should come to him, I will go. I suspect very much that I shall he required to surrender this castle; for the duke of Anjou has marched along the frontiers of his country without entering it, and the count de Foix has long wished for the castle of Malvoisin, in order to be master of Lane-bourg and the frontiers of Bigorre and Comminges. I am ignorant if any treaties have been made between him and the duke of Anjou; but I declare, that as long as I live, I will never surrender the castle of Lourde but to my natural lord the king of England. I therefore order you, brother John, should I appoint you to the command of it, that you swear to me, upon your faith and gentility, you will hold it in the same manner as I do, and that you will never fail in so doing for life or death.'

John took the oath as his brother required, who then set out for Orthès, where on his arrival he dismounted at the hotel of the Moon.

"When he thought it was decent time to wait on the count, he went to him at the castle, who received him most amicably, made him sit at his table, and showed him every mark of attention. Dinner being over, the count said, 'Peter, I have many things to talk with you upon: therefore, you must not go away without my leave.'

"The knight answered, 'My lord, I will cheerfully stay until I have your permission to depart.' The third day the count addressed him, in the presence of the viscount de Gousserant, his brother, the lord d'Anchin in Bigorre, and several knights and squires, and so loud that all heard him:

"'Peter, I have sent for you, to acquaint you, that my lord of Anjou is very angry with me on account of the garrison of Lourde which you command. Through the good offices of some friends I have in his army, my territories have narrowly escaped being overrun; and it is his opinion, and others in his company who hate me, that I support you, because you are of

Béarn. Now I do not wish to incur the anger of so powerful a prince as the duke of Anjon: I therefore command you, under pain of my displeasure, and by the faith and homage you owe me, to give up the castle of Lourde to me.'

"The knight was thunderstruck on hearing this speech, and thought awhile what answer to make: for he perceived the count had spoken in a determined manner. Having fully considered, he said, 'My lord, in truth I owe you faith and homage, for I am a poor knight of your blood and country; but, as for the castle of Lourde, I will never surrender it to you. You have sent for me, and you may therefore do with me as you please. I hold the castle of Lourde from the king of England, who has placed me there; and to no other person but to him will I ever surrender it.'

"The count de Foix, on hearing this answer, was exceedingly wroth, and said, as he drew his dagger, 'Ho, ho! dost thou then say no? By this head, thou hast not said it for nothing.' And, as he uttered these words, he struck him foully with the dagger, so that he wounded him severely in five places, and none of the barons or knights dared to interfere.

The knight replied, 'Ha, ha, my lord, this is not gentle treatment: you have sent, for me hither, and are murdering me.' Having received these five strokes from the dagger, the count ordered him to be cast into the dungeon, which was done; and there he died, for he was ill cured of his wounds."

"Ha, holy Mary," said I to the knight, "was not this a great act of cruelty?"

"Whatever it was," replied he, "so it happened, and ill betide him who angers the count, for then he pardons none. He kept his cousin-german the viscount de Châteaubon, even though he is his heir, eight months prisoner in the tower of the castle

*Jean Froissart kneeling before Gaston III Febus, count of Foix.
(British Library, Royal 14 D V f. 8)*

*http://minos1.bl.uk/catalogues/illuminatedmanuscripts/ILLUMINBi
g.ASP?size=big&IllID=32420*

of Orthès, and then ransomed him for forty thousand francs."

"What, sir," said I, "has not the count de Foix any children ?"

"Eh, in God's name, not in lawful marriage; but he has two young knights, bastards, sir Jenuain and sir Gracien, whom you will see, and whom he loves as well as himself."

"And was he never married?"

"Yes, and is so still, but madame de Foix does not live with him."

"Where does she reside?" "She lives in Navarre, for the king of Navarre is her brother: she was daughter of king Louis of Navarre."

"The count de Foix, had he never any children by her?"

"Yes; a very fine son, who was the delight of his father and of the country: through him the country of Béarn, which is in dispute. would have been settled, for his wife was sister to the count d'Armagnac."

"And pray, sir, may I ask what became of this son?"

"Yes," replied he; "but the story is too long at present, for we are, as you see, arrived at the town."

At these words I left the knight quiet; and we soon after entered Tarbes, where we were very comfortable at the hotel of the Star. We remained there the whole of that day, for it was a commodious place, to refresh ourselves and horses, having good hay, good oats, and a handsome river.

***

On their way to Foix, Sir Espaign du Lyon tells Froissart about the count and his ancestors.

Book III, ch. 8 (Johnes, v. 2, p. 90-94). On the morrow, after mass, having mounted our horses and left Tarbes, we came to Jorre, a town which has always gallantly defended itself against the garrison of Lourde. We passed by it, and entered Béarn, when the knight stopped in the plain, and said, "We are now in Béarn." There were two roads that crossed each other, and we knew not which to take, whether that to Morlens or to Pau: at last, we followed that to Morlens.

In riding over the heaths of Béarn, which are tolerably level, I asked, in order to renew our conversation, "Is the town of Pau near us?"

"Yes," said he, "I will show you the steeple; but it is much farther off than it appears, and the roads are very bad to travel on account of the deep clays, and it would be folly for any one to attempt going through them that is not well acquainted with the country. Below are seated the town and castle of Lourde."

"And who is governor of it now?" "John de Béarn, brother to sir Peter de Béarn that was murdered, and he styles himself séneschal of Bigorre for the king of England."

"Indeed!" said I, "and does this John ever visit the count de Foix?"

"Never since the death of his brother; but his other companions, such as Peter d'Anchin, Ernauton de Restin, Ernauton de Sainte Colombe, and others, go thither, whenever they have occasion."

"Has the countdeFoix made any amends for the murder of the

knight? or has he ever again been in such passions?"

"Yes, very often," replied the knight; "but as for amends, he has never made any, except indeed by secret penances, masses, and prayers: he has with him the son of John de Béarn, a young and courteous squire, whom he greatly loves."

"Holy Mary!" exclaimed I, "since the, duke of Anjou was so desirous to gain Lourde, he ought to be well pleased with the count de Foix, who could murder a knight and his cousin, to accomplish the duke's wishes"

"By my faith, he was so; for soon after the event of his nephew coming to the crown of France, he sent sir Roger d'Espaign and a president of the parliament of Paris, with fair letters patent engrossed and sealed, of the king's declaration that he gave him the county of Bigorre during his life, but that it was necessary he should become liege man and hold it of the crown of France. The count de Foix was very thankful to the king for this mark of his affection, and for the gift of Bigorre, which was unsolicited on his part; but, for anything sir Roger d'Espaign could say or do, he would never accept it. He only retained the castle of Malvoisin, because it was free land, and the castle and its dependencies held of none but God, and formerly had been part of his patrimony. The king of France, to please the duke of Anjou, gave it to the count de Foix; but the count swore he would only hold it on condition never to admit into it any one ill inclined to France; and in truth he had it well guarded. The garrison of Malvoisin would have been as much afraid of the English as any other French or Gascon garrison, but they dared not invade the territories of Foix."

I was much pleased with this history of sir Espaign du Lyon, which I have well remembered; for as soon as we dismounted at our inns, I wrote all down, whether it was late or early, that posterity might have the advantage of it, for there is nothing like writing for the preservation of events.

We rode this morning to Morlens; but, before we arrived, I again began the conversation by saying, "My lord, I have forgotten to ask you, when you were telling me the history of Foix and Armagnac, how the count de Foix was able to dissemble with the duke of Berry, who had married a daughter and sister to the counts d'Armagnac? and if the duke of Berry made war on him, how he behaved?"

"I will tell you: in former times, the duke hated him mortally; but at this moment, by means which you will hear, when at Orthès, they are very good friends."

"My lord, was there any reason for the duke's hatred ?"

"Father of God! no," replied the knight: "I will tell you the cause of it. When Charles king of France, father to the present king, died, the kingdom was divided into two parties respecting its government. My lord of Anjou, who was impatient to go to Italy, and indeed this he afterwards did, took possession of it, and set aside his two brothers the dukes of Berry and Burgundy. The duke of Berry had the government of those parts within the Langue d'Oc, and the duke of Burgundy of the Langue d'Ouy and all Picardy.

"When the inhabitants of Languedoc heard that my lord of Berry was to govern them they were much alarmed, especially those of Toulouse and its dependencies; for they knew the duke to he a spendthrift, who would get money any way he could, without caring how he oppressed the people. Some Bretons still remained in the Toulousain, Carcassonnois and Rouergue, whom the duke of Anjou had left, and they pillaged the whole country: it was reported the duke of Berry supported them, in order to be master of the principal towns. The duke himself was not at the time I am speaking of in

Languedoc, but attending the king in the wars in Flanders.

"The citizens of Toulouse, who are a powerful body, perceiving how young the king was and how much occupied with the affairs of his uncle the duke of Burgundy in Flanders, and that they were perpetually plundered by Bretons and other pillagers, so that they knew not how to prevent it, sent to the count de Foix offers of paying him a certain sum monthly, if he would undertake the government and defence of their city and the other neighbouring towns. They entreated him very earnestly comply with their request, because they knew him to be an upright man, a great lover of justice, fortunate in his affairs, and much feared by his enemies. The inhabitants of Toulouse have always borne him great affection, for he has ever been a good neighbour to them.

"He undertook the charge of their government, and swore to hold and defend the country in its right against all who were ill inclined, with the reservation of the rights of the king of France. He instantly ordered considerable detachments of men at arms on the different Toads The pillagers used to take; and one day he had hanged or drowned upwards of four hundred of them at Robesten in the Toulousain, which gained him so much the love of those of Toulouse, Carcassonne, Beziers, Montpelier and the other towns, that it was reported Languedoc had revolted and chosen for its lord the count de Foix.

"The duke of Berry, who had the government of it, was ill pleased at this intelligence, and conceived a great hatred to the count de Foix, for interfering so much in the affairs of France, and for his supporting the people of Toulouse in their revolt. He ordered men at arms into that country, but they were severely repulsed by the partisans of the count de Foix, and were forced to retreat, or they would have suffered for it. This angered the duke still more: he said the count de Foix was the proudest and most presumptuous man in the world; and he would not suffer his name to be mentioned with praise in his presence; but he did not make war against him, for the count had all his towns and castles so well garrisoned, none dared to invade his territories.

"When the duke of Berry entered Languedoc, the count resigned the government, and would not any way meddle, in prejudice to the duke; but his dislike still continued as great as ever. I will now say a word of the means that established peace between them.

"About ten years ago, Eleanor de Comminges (at present countess of Boulogne, a near relation to the countdeFoix, and lawful heiress to the county of Comminges, notwithstanding the count d'Armagnac was in possession) came to the count de Foix at Orthès, bringing with her a young girl, three years old. The count entertained her handsomely, inquired her business, whence she came, and whither going?

"'My lord,' said she, ' I am going to my uncle and aunt-in-law, the count and countess de Durgueil, in Arragon, there to remain; for I have much displeasure in living with my husband, sir John de Boulogne, son of the count de Boulogne. I expected he would have recovered for me mine inheritance of Comminges from the count d'Armagnac, who not only keeps it, but has confined my sister in prison; but my husband is too soft a knight, whose sole delight is eating and drinking, and enjoying Isis pleasures; and the moment his father dies, he will sell the greater part of his estates to multiply his luxuries: it is for these reasons I cannot live with him.

"'I have also brought my daughter with me, whom I deliver up to your charge, and appoint you her guardian, to instruct and defend her; for I well know that, from our relationship, you will not disappoint me; and I have the greatest confidence in the care you will take of my daughter Joan. It was with much difficulty I could get her from her father's hands, and out of the country; but as I know the Armagnacs, your adversaries as well as mine, are capable of carrying her off, being the true heiress of Comminges, I deliver her to you; therefore do not fail me in this business, I entreat of you; for I firmly believe, that when my husband shall know I left her under your care, he will be pleased, having frequently said, that this girl would give hint much trouble.'

"The count de Foix was delighted to hear his cousin, the lady Eleanor, thus talk, and thought in his own mind (for he has a very fertile imagination), that this girl was brought to him very opportunely, as by her means he could make a stable peace with his enemies, or marry her so nobly they would fear him.

"He answered,' Madam and cousin, I will most cheerfully comply with your request: I am bounden to it by our relationship. With regard to your daughter, I will defend, and be as careful of her as if she were my own child.'

"'A thousand thanks, my lord,' said the lady. Thus did the young lady of Boulogne remain with the count at his house in Orthès, which she has never since quitted, and the lady her mother pursued her journey to Arragon. She has returned to see her two or three times, but has never asked to have her back; for the count acquits himself towards her as if she were indeed his own child. But I must tell you the means by which, if formerly he was in the ill graces of the duke de Berry, he is now on good terms. The duke at this moment is very desirous to marry her; and from what I heard at Avignon from the pope, who spoke to me on the subject, and who is cousin-german to her father, the duke will employ him to ask for him, as he is determined to make her his wife."

"By holy Mary," said I to the knight, "your history has given me much pleasure and done me service: you shall not lose a word you have said, for they shall all be chronicled with every thing I say and do, if God grant me health to return again to Valenciennes, of which place I am a native; but I am very angry at one thing."

"What is that?" said the knight.

"On my faith, it is, that so noble and valiant a prince as the count de Foix should not have any legal heirs by his wife."

"Please God he had," replied the knight; "for if his child were now alive, he would be the happiest lord in the world, and his vassals be equally rejoiced."

"What!" said I, "will his estates be without an heir?"

"Oh, no: the viscount de Châteaubon, his cousin-german, is his heir." "Is he a valiant man at arms?"

"God help him! no; and for that reason the count de Foix cannot bear him. He will make his two bastard-sons, who are young and handsome knights, his heirs, and intends to connect them very highly by marriage; for he has money enough, which will find them wives to uphold and assist them."

"Sir," said I, "all this is very well; but I do not think it just nor decent that bastards should inherit lands."

"Why not?" added he, "if proper heirs be wanting. Do not you see how the Spaniards crowned for king the bastard don Henry? and the Portuguese have done the same thing. It has frequently happened that bastards have gained possession of several kingdoms by force. Was not William the Conqueror bastard-son of a duke of Normandy! He won all England, as well as the king's daughter who then governed, and was himself king, and from him all the kings of England are descended."

Well, sir," said I, "all this may be well, for there is nothing but what may happen. Surely those of the Armagnac party are too strong and this country must always be at war. Tell me, my dear sir, the first origin of the wars between Foix and Armagnac, and which had the fairest cause."

"That I will, by my faith," answered the knight : "It has, however, been a wonderful war, for each thinks he has justice on his side. You must know, that formerly, I imagine about one hundred years from this time, there was a lord of Béarn called Gaston, a most gallant man at arms: he was buried with great solemnity in the church of the Frères Mineurs, at Orthès, where you will find him and may see of what a size he was in body and limbs, for during his lifetime he had a handsome resemblance made of him, in brass. This Gaston had two daughters; the eldest of whom he married to the count d'Armagnac of that period, and the youngest to the count de Foix, nephew to the king of Arragon. The counts de Foix still bear those arms (for they are descended from the kings of Arragon), which are paly or and gules; and this, I believe, you know. It happened that the lord of Béarn had a severe and long war with the king of Castille of that time, who, marching through Biscay with a numerous army, entered Béarn. Sir Gaston de Béarn, having intelligence of his march, collected people from all quarters, and had written to his two sons-in-law, the counts d'Armagnac and de Foix, to come with all quickness with their forces, to assist him in the defence and preservation of his inheritance.

"On the arrival of these letters, the count de Foix assembled his vassals as speedily as possible, and sent for assistance to

*An English herald approaches Scottish soldiers; detail from an
illustrated edition of Froissart's Chronicles*

*Scanned from The Story Of Scotland, First Press and Scottish Daily
Record Group, 1999-2000*

all his friends. He exerted himself so effectually that he collected five hundred knights and squires and two thousand footmen armed with javelins, darts and shields: accompanied by these, he marched into Béarn to assist the lord his father, who was much delighted therewith. This army crossed the river Bane by the bridge of Orthès, and took up their quarters between Sauveterre and l'Hôpital. The king of Castille, with full twenty thousand men, was encamped not far from them. Sir Gaston de Béarn and the count de Foix, expecting the count d'Armagnac, waited for him three days: on the fourth a herald arrived from the count d'Armagnac with letters to sir Gaston, to say he could not come, and that it was not agreeable to him to arm in behalf of the country of Béarn, for at present he had not any interest in it.

"Sir Gaston, perceiving he was not to have any assistance from the count d'Armagnac, was much astonished, and asked the count de Foix and the barons of Béarn, how he should act:

"'My lord,' replied the count de Foix, since we are assembled, we will offer battle to your enemies.' This advice was followed, and instantly they all armed: they might be about twelve hundred men with helmets, and six thousand on foot.

"The count de Foix, with the van division, charged the king of Castille and his army in their quarters. The battle was very severe and bloody: upwards of two thousand Castillians were slain. The count de Foix made prisoners the son and brother of the king of Castille, whom he sent to sir Gaston de Béarn, who commanded the rear division. The Castillians were completely defeated. The count de Foix pursued them as far as the gates of Saint Andero in Biscay, where the king took refuge in an abbey, and put on a monk's frock, otherwise he would have been taken: those saved themselves who could, on board of vessels. The count de Foix, on his return to sir Gaston de Béarn, was received by him with much joy, as indeed he had reason, for he had saved his honour and secured the country, which otherwise would have been lost. This battle and defeat of the Castillians, and the capture of the son and brother of the king, induced him to accede to a peace with the lord de Béarn on such terms as he dictated.

"Sir Gaston de Béarn, on his return to Orthès, in the presence of all the knights of Béarn and Foix, took the count de Foix by the hand and said: Fair son, you are indeed my son, my loyal son, and have secured for ever my honour and the honour of my country. The count d'Armagnac, who married my eldest daughter, has excused himself from assisting in the defence of my inheritance, in which he was so much interested. I therefore declare that he has forfeited and shall lose whatever share he may have expected from it in behalf of my daughter. You, count de Foix, shall inherit the whole of my territory of Béarn after my decease, you and your heirs for ever. I entreat and command all my subjects to agree with me, and to seal this gift, which I present to you, my fair son of Foix.'

"All present answered 'My lord, we will most cheerfully do so.'

"Thus did the former counts de Foix become lords of Béarn: they bear the arms and the name, and have the war-cry and profit. However, the Armagnacs have not the less urged their claims to those rights they say they are entitled to; and this is the cause of the quarrel and war between Armagnac, Foix and Béarn."

By my faith," said I to the knight, "you have perfectly well explained the matter. I never before heard any thing of it, but, since I now do, I will perpetuate it, if God grant that I return to my own country. But there is one thing more I could wish to know: what caused the death of the son of the count de Foix?"

The knight became pensive, and said "It is too melancholy a subject: I therefore wish not to speak of it; but when you are at Orthès, if you ask, you will find many there who will tell you the whole history." I was obliged to content myself with this answer; so we continued our journey until we arrived at Morlens.

***

Sir Espaign du Lyon brings Froissart at last to the count of Foix's court.

Book III, ch. 9 (Johnes, v. 2, pp. 94-95). On the morrow we set out, and dined at Montgerbal, when having remounted, and drank a cup at Ercie, we arrived by sunset at Orthès. The knight dismounted at his own house: and I did the same at the hôtel of the Moon, kept by a squire of the count, called Ernauton du Pin, who received me with much pleasure on account of my being a Frenchman. Sir Espaign du Lyon, who had accompanied me, went to the castle, to speak with the count on his affairs: he found him in his gallery, for a little before that hour he had dined. It was a custom with the count, which he had followed from his infancy, to rise at noon and sup at midnight.

The knight informed him of my arrival, and I was instantly sent for; for he is a lord above all others who delights to see strangers, in order to hear news. On my entering, he received me handsomely, and retained me of his household, where I staid upwards of twelve weeks well entertained, as were my horses. Our acquaintance was strengthened by my having brought with me a book which I had made at the desire of Winceslaus of Bohemia, duke of Luxembourg and Brabant. In this book, called le Meliador, are contained all the songs, ballads, roundelays and virelays, which that gentle duke had composed, and of them I had made this collection. Every night after supper I read out to him parts: during which time neither he nor any one else spoke, for he was desirous I should be well heard, and took much delight in it. When any passages were not perfectly clear, he himself discussed them with me, not in his Gascon language, but in very good French.

I shall relate to you several things respecting him and his household, for I tarried there as long as I could gain any information. Count Gaston Phoebus de Foix, of whom I am now speaking, was at that time fifty-nine years old; and I must say, that although I have seen very many knights, kings, princes and others, I have never seen any so handsome, either in the form of his limbs and shape, or in countenance, which was fair and ruddy, with grey and amorous eyes, that gave delight whenever he chose to express affection. He was so perfectly formed, one could not praise him too much. He loved earnestly the things he ought to love, and hated those which it was becoming him so to hate. He was a prudent knight, full of enterprise and wisdom. He had never any men of abandoned character with him, reigned prudently, and was constant in his devotions. There were regular nocturnals from the Psalter, prayers from the rituals to the Virgin, to the Holy Ghost, and from the burial service. He had every day distributed as alms, at his gate, five forms in small coin, to all comers. He was liberal and courteous in his gifts; and well knew how to take when it was proper, and to give back where he had confidence.

He mightily loved dogs above all other animals; and during the summer and winter amused himself much with hunting. He never liked any foolish works nor ridiculous extravagancies; and would know every month the amount of his expenditure. He chose from his own subjects twelve of the most able to receive and administer his finances: two of them had the management for two months, when they were changed for two others; and from them he selected one as comptroller, in whom he placed his greatest confidence, and to whom all the others rendered their accounts. This comptroller accounted by rolls or written books, which were laid before the count. He had certain coffers in his apartment, from whence he took money to give to different knights, squires or gentlemen, when they cause to wait on him, for none ever left him without a gift; and these sums he continually increased, in order to be prepared for any event that might happen. He was easy of access to all, and entered very freely into discourse, though laconic in his advice and in his answers. He employed four secretaries to write and copy his letters; and these secretaries were obliged to be in readiness the moment he came out from his closet. He called them neither John, Walter, nor William, but his good-for-nothings, to whom he gave his letters after he had read them, either to copy, or to do any thing else he miglst command.

In such manner did the count de Foix live. When he quitted his chamber at midnight for supper, twelve servants bore each a large lighted torch before him, which were placed near his table and gave a brilliant light to the apartment. The hall was full of knights and squires; and there were plenty of tables laid out for any person who chose to sup. No one spoke to him at his table, unless he first began a conversation. He commonly ate heartily of poultry, but only the wings and thighs; for in the day-time, he neither ate nor drank much. He had great pleasure in hearing minstrels, as he himself was a proficient in the science, and made his secretaries sing songs, ballads and roundelays. He remained at table about two hours; and was pleased when fanciful dishes were served up to him, which having seen, he immediately sent them to the tables of his knights and squires.

In short, everything considered, though I had before been in several courts of kings, dukes, princes, counts, and noble ladies, I was never at one which pleased me more, nor was I ever more delighted with feats of arms, than at this of the count de Foix. There were knights and squires to be seen in every chamber, hall and court, going backwards and forwards, and conversing on arms and amours. Every thing honourable was there to be found. All intelligence from distant countries was there to be learnt; for the gallantry of the count had brought visitors from all parts of the world. It was there I was informed of the greater part of those events which had happened in Spain, Portugal, Arragon, Navarre, England, Scotland, and on the borders of Languedoc; for I saw, during my residence, knights aisd squires arrive from every nation. I therefore made inquiries from them, or from the count himself, who cheerfully conversed with me.

***

The death of the count de Foix's son.

Book III, ch. 9 (Johnes, v. 2, pp. 95-99). I was very anxious to know, seeing the hôtel of the count so spacious and so amply supplied, what was become of his son Gaston, and by what accident he had died, for sir Espaign du Lyon would never satisfy my curiosity. I made so many inquiries, that at last an old and intelligent squire informed me. He thus began his tale: --"It is well known that the count and countess de Foix are not on good terms with each other, nor have they been so for a long time. This dissension arose from the king of Navarre, who is the lady's brother. The king of Navarre had offered to pledge himself for the lord d'Albreth, whom the count de Foix held in prison, in the sum of fifty thousand francs.

"The count de Foix, knowing the king of Navarre to be crafty and faithless, would not accept his security, which piqued the countess, and raised her indignation against her husband: she said, "My lord, you show but little confidence in the honour of my brother, the king of Navarre, when you will not trust him for fifty thousand francs: if you never gain more from the Armagnacs and Labrissiens than you have done, you ought to be contented: you know that you are to assign over my dower, which amounts to fifty thousand francs, into the hands of my brother: therefore you cannot run any risk for the repayment.'

"'Lady, you say truly,' replied the count; ' but, if I thought the king of Navarre would stop the payment for that cause, the lord d'Albreth should never leave Orthès until he had paid me the utmost farthing. Since, however, you entreat it, it shall be done, not out of love to you, but out of affection to my son.' Upon this, and from the assurance of the king of Navarre, who acknowledged himself debtor to the count de Foix, the lord d'Albreth recovered his liberty: He turned to the French interest, and married the sister of the duke of Bourbon. He paid, at his convenience, to the king of Navarre the sum of fifty thousand francs, according to his obligation; but that king never repaid them to the count de Foix.

"The count on this said to his wife, 'Lady, you must go to your brother in Navarre, and tell him that I am very ill satisfied with him for withholding from me the sum he has received on my account.'

"The lady replied, she would cheerfully go thither, and set out from Orthès with her attendants. On her arrival at Pampeluna, her brother the king of Navarre received her with much joy. The lady punctually delivered her message, which when the king had heard, he replied, 'My fair sister, the money is yours, as your dower from the count de Foix; and, since I have possession of it, it shall never go out of the kingdom of Navarre.'

"'Ah, my lord,' replied the lady, 'you will by this create a great hatred between the count de Foix and me; and, if you persist in this resolution, I shall never dare return, for my lord will put me to death for having deceived him.'

"' I cannot say,' answered the king, who was unwilling to let such a sum go out of his hands, 'how you should act, whether to remain or return; but as I have possession of the money, and it is my right to keep it for you, it shall never leave Navarre.'

"The countess de Foix, not being able to obtain any other answer, remained in Navarre, not daring to return home. The count de Foix, perceiving the malice of the king of Navarre, began to detest his wife, though she was no way to blame, for not returning after she had delivered his message. In truth, she was afraid; for she knew her husband to be cruel when displeased with any one. Thins things remained. Gaston, the son of my lord, grew up, and became a fine young gentleman. He was married to the daughter of the count d'Armagnac, sister to the present count and to sir Bernard d'Armagnac; and by this union peace was insured between Foix and Armagnac. The youths might be about fifteen or sixteen years old: he was a   very   handsome figure, and the exact resemblance to his father in his whole form.

"He took it into his head to make a journey into Navarre, to visit his mother and uncle; but it was an unfortunate journey for him and for this country. On his arrival in Navarre, he was splendidly entertained : and he staid some time with his mother. On taking leave, he could not prevail on her, notwithstanding his remonstrances and entreaties, to accompany him back; for, the lady having asked if the count de Foix his father had ordered him to bring her back, he replied, that when he set out, no such orders had been given, which caused her to fear trusting herself with him.

"She therefore remained, and the heir of Foix went to Pampeluna to take leave of his uncle. The king entertained him well, and detained him upwards of ten days: on his departure, he made him handsome presents, and did the same by his attendants. The last gift the king gave him was the cause of his death, and I will tell you how it happened.

"As the youth was on the point of setting out, the king took him privately into his chamber, and gave him a bag full of powder, which was of such pernicious quality as would cause the death of any one that ate of it. 'Gaston, my fair nephew,' said the king, 'will you do what I am about to tell you? You see how unjustly the count de Foix hates your mother, who being my sister, it displeases me as much as it should you. If you wish to reconcile your father to your mother, you must take a small pinch of this powder, and when you see a proper opportunity, strew it over the meat destined for your father's table; but, take care no one sees you. The instant he shall have tasted it, he will be impatient for his wife, your mother, to return to hun, and they will love each other henceforward so strongly they will never again be separated. You ought to be anxious to see this accomplished. Do not tell it to any one: for, if you do, it will lose its effect.'

The youth, who believed everything his uncle the king of Navarre had told him, replied, he would cheerfully do as lie had said; and on this he departed from Pampeluna, on his return to Orthès. His father the count de Foix received him with pleasure, and asked what was the news in Navarre, and what presents and jewels had been given him; he replied, 'Very handsome ones,' and showed them all, except the bag which contained the powder.

"It was customary, in the hotel de Foix, for Gaston and his bastard brother Evan to sleep in the same chamber: they

Chroniques

By Loyset Liédet, 15th century

mutually loved each other and were dressed alike, for they were nearly of the same size and age. It fell out, that their clothes were once mixed together; and, the coat of Gaston being on the bed, Evan, who was malicious enough, noticing the powder in the bag, said to Gaston, 'What is this that you wear every day on your breast?'

"Gaston was not pleased at the question, and replied, 'Give me back my coat, Evan: you have nothing to do with it.' Evan flung him his coat, which Gaston put on, but was very pensive the whole day. Three days after, as if God was desirous of saving the life of the count de Foix, Gaston quarrelled with Evan at tennis, and gave him a box on the ear. The boy was vexed at this, and ran crying to the apartment of the count, who had just heard mass. The count, on seeing him in tears, asked what was thin matter.

"'In God's name, my lord,' replied Evan, 'Gaston has beaten me, but he deserves beating much more than I do.'

"'For what reason?' said the count, who began to have some suspicions.

"'On my faith,' said Evan, 'ever since his return from Navarre, he wears on his breast a bag of powder: I know not what use it can be of, nor what he intends to do with it; except that he has once or twice told me, his mother would soon return hither, and be more in your good graces than ever she was.'

"'Ho,' said the count, 'hold thy tongue, and be sure thou do not mention what thou hast just told me to any man breathing.'

"'My lord,' replied the youth, 'I will obey you.'

"The count de Foix was very thoughtful on this subject, and remained alone until dinner-time, when he rose up, and seated himself as usual at his table in the hall. His son Gaston always placed the dishes before him, and tasted the meats. As soon as he had served the first dish, and done what was usual, the count cast his eyes on him, having formed his plan, and saw the strings of the bag hanging from his pourpoint. This sight made his blood boil, and he said, 'Gaston, come hither: I want to whisper you something.'

"The youth advanced to the table, when the count, opening his bosom, undid his pourpoint, and with his knife cut away the bag. The young man was thunderstruck and said not a word, but turned pale with fear, and began to tremble exceedingly, for he was conscious he had done wrong. The count opened the bag, took some of the powder, which he strewed over a slice of bread, and, calling a dog to him, gave it him to eat. The instant the dog had eaten a morsel his eyes rolled round in his head, and he died.

The count on this was very wroth, and indeed had reason: rising from table, he would have struck his son with a knife; but the knights and squires rushed in between them, saying, 'For God's sake, my lord, do not be too hasty, but make further inquiries before you do any ill to your son.'

"The first words the count uttered were in Gascon; 'Ho, Gaston, thou traitor! for thee, and to increase thy inheritance which would have come to thee, have I made war, and incurred the hatred of the kings of France, England, Spain, Navarre, and Arragon, and have borne myself gallantly against them, and thou wishest to murder me! Thy disposition must be infamously bad: know therefore thou shalt die with this blow.' And leaping over the table with a knife in his hand, he would have slain him: but the knights and squires again interfered, and on their knees said to him with tears, 'Ah, ah! my lord, for Heaven's sake, do not kill Gaston: you have no other child. Let him be confined and inquire further into the business. Perhaps he was ignorant what was in the bag, and may therefore be blameless.'

"'Well,' replied the count, 'let him be confined in the dungeon, but so safely guarded that he may be forthcoming.'

"The youth was therefore confined in this tower. The count had many of those who served his son arrested, but not all; for several escaped out of the country: in particular, the bishop of Lescar, who was much suspected, as were several others. He put to death not less than fifteen, after they had suffered the torture; and the reason he gave was, that it was impossible but they must have been acquainted with the secrets of his son, and they ought to have informed him by saying, 'My lord, Gaston wears constantly on his breast a bag of such and such a form.' This they did not do, and suffered a terrible death for it; which was a pity, for there were not in all Gascony such handsome or well-appointed squires. The household of the count de Foix was always splendidly established.

"This business went to the heart of the count, as he plainly showed; for he assembled at Orthès all the nobles and prelates of Foix and Béarn, and others the principal persons of the country. When they were met, he informed them of the cause of his calling them together, and told them how culpable he had found Gaston; insomuch that it was his intention he should be put to death, as he thought him deserving of it.

"They unanimously replied to this speech,' My lord, saving your grace's favour, we will not that Gaston be put to death: he is your heir and you have none other.' When the count thus heard his subjects declare their sentiments in favour of his son, he hesitated, and thought he might sufficiently chastise him by two or three months' confinement, when he would send him on his travels for a few years until his ill conduct should be forgotten, and he feel grateful for the lenity of his punishment. He therefore dissolved the meeting; but those of Foix would not quit Orthès until the count had assured them Gaston should not be put to death, so great was their affection to him. He complied with their request, but said he would keep him some time in prison. On this promise, those who had been assembled departed, and Gaston remained a prisoner in Orthès.

"News of this was spread far and near, and reached pope Gregory XI. who resided at Avignon: he sent instantly the cardinal of Amiens, as his legate, to Béarn, to accommodate this affair; but he had scarcely travelled as far as Beziers, when he heard he had no need to continue his journey, for that Gaston the son of the count de Foix was dead.

"I will tell you the cause of his death, since I have said so much on the subject. The count de Foix had caused him to be confined in a room of the dungeon where was little light: there lie remained for ten days. He scarcely ate or drank anything of the food which was regularly brought to him, but threw it aside. It is said, that after his deaths, all the meat was found untouched, so that it is marvellous how he could have lived so long. The count would not permit any one to remain in the chamber to advise or comfort him: he therefore never put off the clothes he had on when he entered his prison. This made him melancholy and vexed him, for he did not expect so much harshness: he therefore cursed the hour he was born, and lamented that he should come to such an end.

"On the day of his death, those who brought him food said, 'Gaston, here is meat for you.' He paid not any attention to it, but said, 'Put it down.' The person who served him, looking about, saw all the meat untouched that he had brought thither the last days: then, shutting the door, he went to the count and said, 'My lord, for God's sake, look to your son: he is starving himself in his prison. I do not believe he has eaten anything since his confinement; for I see all that I have carried to him lying on one side untouched.'

On hearing this, the count was enraged, and, without saying a word, left his apartment and went to the prison of his son. In an evil hour, he had in his hand a knife, with which he had been paring and cleaning his nails, he held it by the blade so closely that scarcely the thickness of a groat appeared of the point, when, pushing aside the tapestry that covered the entrance of the prison, through ill luck, he hit his son on a vein of his throat, as he uttered, 'Ha, traitor, why dost not thou eat?' and instantly left the room, without saying or doing anything more. The youth was much frightened at his father's arrival, and withal exceedingly weak from fasting. The point of the knife, small as it was, cut a vein, which as soon as he felt he turned himself on one side and died.

"The count had barely got back again to his apartment when the attendants of his son came and said, 'My lord, Gaston is dead.'

"'Dead!' cried the count.

"'Yes, God help me! indeed he is, my lord.' The count would not believe it, and sent one of his knights to see. The knight, on his return, confirmed the news.

The count was now bitterly affected, and cried out, 'Ha, ha, Gaston! what a sorry business has this turned out for thee and me! In an evil hour didst thou go to visit thy mother in Navarre. Never shall I again enjoy the happiness I had formerly.'

He then ordered his barber to be sent for, and was shaven quite bare: he clothed himself, as well as his whole household, in black. The body of the youth was borne, with tears and lamentations, to the church of the Augustin friars at Orthès, where it was buried. Thus have I related to you the death of Gaston de Foix: his father killed him indeed, but the king of Navarre was the cause of this sad event."

My heart was much affected at this recital of the squire of Béarn relative to the deaths of Gaston; and I was truly sorry for the count his father, whom I found a magnificent, generous, and courteous lord, and also for the country that was discontented for want of an heir. I then took leave of the squire, after having thanked him for the pleasure his narration had given me.

***

A squire at the count de Foix's court tells Froissart another story.

Book III, ch. 9 (Johnes, v. 2, pp. 99-100). I saw him frequently afterwards in the hôtel de Foix, when we had always some conversation. I once asked him about sir Peter de Béarn, bastard-brother to the count, who seemed to me a knight of great valour, and if he were rich or married. "Married indeed he is," replied he, "but neither his wife nor children live with him."

"For what reason?" said I.

"I will tell you," replied the squire.

"Sir Peter de Béarn has a custom, when asleep in the night-time, to rise, arm himself, draw his sword, and to begin fighting as if he were in actual combat. The chamberlains and valets who sleep in his chamber to watch him, on hearing him rise, go to him, and inform him what he is doing: of all which, he tells them, he is quite ignorant, and that they lie.

Sometimes they leave neither arms nor sword in his chamber, when he makes such a noise and clatter as if all the devils in hell were there. They therefore think it best to replace the arms, and sometimes he forgets them, and remains quietly in his bed."

I again asked, if he had a large fortune with his wife.

"Yes, in God's name had he," says the squire; " but the lady keeps possession of it, and enjoys the profits, except a fourth part, which sir Peter has."

"And where does his lady reside?"

"She lives with her cousin the king of Castille: her father was count of Biscay and cousin-german to don Pedro, who put him to death. lie wanted also to hay hands on this lady, to confine her. He seized her hands, and as long as he lived she received nothing from them. It was told her, when, by the deaths of her father, she became countess of Biscay,' Lady, save yourself; for if don Pedro lay hands on you, he will put you to death, or at least imprison you, for he is much enraged that you should say he strangled his queen, sister to the duke of Bourbon and the queen of France, in her bed; and your evidence is more readily believed than any other, for you were of her bed-chamber.' For this reason, the countess Florence de Biscaye quitted the country with few attendants, as one naturally wishes to fly from death, passed through Biscay and came hither, when she told my lord her history.

"The count, who is kind and affectionate to all ladies and damsels, had compassion on her, detained her at his court, and placed her with the lady de la Karasse, a great baroness of this country, and provided her with all things suitable to her rank. Sir Peter de Béarn, his brother, was at that time a young knight, and had not then this custom of fighting in his sleep, but was much in the good graces of the count, who concluded a marriage for him with this lady, and recovered her lands from don Pedro. She has a son and daughter by sir Peter, but they are young, and with her in Castille, for she would not leave them with their father; and she has the right of enjoying the greater part of her own lands."

"Holy Mary!" said I to the squire, "how came the knight. to have such fancies, that he cannot sleep quietly in bed, but must rise and skirmish about the house! this is very strange."

"By my faith," answered the squire, "they have frequently asked him, but he knows nothing about it. Thin first time it happened, was on the night following a day when he had hunted a wonderfully large bear in the woods of Béarn. This bear had killed four of his dogs and wounded many more, so that the others were afraid of him; upon which sir Peter drew his sword of Bordeaux steel, and advanced on the bear with great rage, on account of the loss of his dogs: he combated him a long time with much bodily danger, and with great, difficulty slew him, when he returned to his castle of Languedudon, in Biscay, and had the bear carried with him. Every one was astonished at the enormous size of the beast, and the courage of the knight who had attacked and slain it.

"When the countess of Biscay, his wife, saw the bear, she instantly fainted, and was carried to her chamber, where she continued very disconsolate all that and the following day, and would not say what ailed her. On the third day she told her husband 'she should never recover her health until she had made a pilgrimage to St. James's shrine at Compostella. Give me leave, therefore, to go thither, and to carry my son Peter and my daughter Adrienne with me: I request it of you.' Sir Peter too easily complied: she had packed up all her jewels and plate unobserved by any one; for she had resolved never to return again.

The lady set out on her pilgrimage, and took that opportunity of visiting her cousins the king and queen of Castille, who entertained her handsomely. She is still with them, and will neither return herself nor send her children. The same night he had hunted and killed the hear, this custom of walking in his sleep seized him.

"It is rumoured, the lady was afraid of something unfortunate happening, the moment she saw the bear, and this caused her fainting; for that her father once hunted this hear, and during the chace, a voice cried out, though he saw nobody, 'Thou huntest me: yet I wish thee no ill; but thou shalt die a miserable death.' The lady remembered this when she saw time bear, as well as that her father had been beheaded by don Pedro without any cause; and she maintains that something unfortunate will happen to her husband; and that what passes now is nothing to what will come to pass. I have told you the story of sir Peter de Béarn," said the squire, "in compliance with your wishes: it is a well-known fact; and what do you think of it?"

I was very pensive at the wonderful things I had heard, and replied, "I do believe everything you have said: we find in ancient authors how gods and goddesses formerly changed men into beasts, according to their pleasure, and women also into birds. This bear, therefore, might have been a knight hunting in the forest of Biscay, when he, perchance, angered some god or goddess, who changed him into a bear, to do penance, as Acteon was transformed into a stag"

"Acteon!" cried the squire: " my good sir, do relate it, for I shall be very happy to listen to you."

"According to ancient authors, we read that Acteon was a

The men of Ghent capture and pillage Grammont (1380). (BNF, FR 2644) Jean Froissart, Chronicles, fol. 135 Flandres, Bruges 15th Century. (185 x 200 mm)

handsome and accomplished knight, who loved dogs and the chase above all things. He was once hunting a stag of a prodigious size: the chase lasted the whole day, when he lost his men and his hounds; but, eager in pursuing the stag, he came to a large meadow, surrounded by high trees, in which was a fountain, where the goddess of Chastity and her nymphs were bathing themselves. The knight came upon them so suddenly that they were not aware of him, and he had advanced so far he could not retreat.

"The nymphs, in their fright, ran to cover their mistress, whose modesty was wounded at thus being seen naked. She viewed the knight over the heads of her attendants, and said. 'Acteon, whoever has sent thee hither has no great love for thee: I will not, that when thou shalt go hence, thou brag of having seen me naked, as well as my nymphs; and for the outrage thou hast committed, thou shalt perform a penance. I change thee, therefore, into the form of the stag thou hast this day hunted.' He was instantly transformed into a stag, who naturally loves waters.

"Thus it may have happened with regard to the bear whose history you have told me, and the countess may have had some knowledge or some fears which at the moment she would not discover: she therefore ought to be excused for what she has done." The squire answered, " It may perchance be so;" and thus ended our conversation.

***

During a prolonged visit at the court of the Count of Foix, Froissart meets and speaks to many men-at-arms.

Book III, ch. 10 (Johnes, v. II, pp. 101-8). To speak briefly and truly, the count de Foix was perfect in person and in mind; and no contemporary prince could be compared with him for sense, honour, or liberality. At the feasts of Christmas, which he kept with great solemnity, crowds of knights and squires from Gascony waited on him, to all of whom he gave splendid entertainments. I saw there the bourg d'Espaign, of whose surprising strength sir Espaign du Lyon had told me, which made me more desirous to see him, and the count showed him many civilities. I saw also knights from Arragon and England; which last were of the household of the duke of Lancaster, who at that time resided at Bordeaux, whom the count received very graciously, and presented with handsome gifts.

I made acquaintance with these knights, and by them was informed of several things which had happened in Castille, Navarre, and Portugal, which I shall clearly detail in proper time and place.

I saw there also a Gascon squire, called le Bascot de Mauléon, an expert man at arms, and about fifty years old, according to his appearance. He arrived at the hotel of the Moon, where I lodged with Ernauton du Pin, in grand array, having led horses with him like to a great baron, and he and his attendants were served on plate of gold and silver. When I heard his name, and saw how much respect the count de Foix and all the others paid him, I asked sir Espaign du Lyon, "Is not this the squire who quitted the castle of Trigalet, when the duke of Anjou lay before Mauvoisin?" Yes," replied he; "and he is as able a captain and as good a man at arms as any existing." Upon this I besought his acquaintance, as he was lodged in the same hotel as myself, with a cousin of his, a Gascon, called Arnauton, governor of Garlat in Auvergne, whom I well knew, and who assisted me in it, as did also the bourg de Copaire.

One night, as we were sitting round the fire chatting and waiting for midnight, which was the hour the count supped, his cousin began a conversation relative to his former life, and asked him to tell his adventures and success in arms, without concealing loss or profit, as he knew he could well remember them. Upon this he said, " Sir John, have you in your chronicle what I am going to speak of?" "I do not know," replied I; " but begin your story, which I shall be happy to hear; for I cannot recollect every particular of my history, nor can I have been perfectly informed of every event." "That is true," added the squire, and then began his history in these words:

"The first time I bore arms was under the captal de Buch at the battle of Poitiers: by good luck I made that day three prisoners, a knight and two squires, who paid me, one with the other, four thousand francs. The following year I was in Prussia with the count de Foix and his cousin the captal, under whose command I was. On our return, we found the duchess of Normandy, the duchess of Orleans, and a great number of ladies and damsels, shut up in Meaux in Brie. The peasants had confined them in the market-place of Meaux, and would have violated them, if God had not sent us thither: for they were completely in their power, as they amounted to more than ten thousand, and the ladies were alone. Upwards of six thousand Jacks were killed on the spot, and they never afterwards rebelled.

"At this time there was a truce between the kings of France and England, but the king of Navarre continued the war on his own personal quarrel with the regent of France. The count de Foix returned to his own country, but my master and self remained with the king of Navarre and in his pay. We made, with the help of others, a severe war on France; particularly in Picardy, where we took many towns and castles in the bishoprics of Beauvois and Amiens: we were masters of the country and rivers, and gained very large sums of money.

When the truce expired between France and England, the king of Navarre discontinued his war, as peace had been made between him and the regent. The king of England crossed the sea with a large army, and laid siege to Rheims, whither he sent for the captal, who at that time was at Clermont in Beauvolsis, carrying on the war on his own account. We joined the king of England and his children. But," said the squire, "I fancy you must have written all this, and how the king of England broke up his siege through famine, and how he came before Chartres, and how peace was made between the two kings." "That is true," replied I: " I have all this, as well as the treaties which were then concluded."

Upon this Bascot de Mauléon thus continued his narration.

"This treaty of peace being concluded, it was necessary for all men at arms and free companies, according to the words of the treaty, to evacuate the fortresses or castles they held. Great numbers collected together, with many poor companions who had learnt the art of war under different commanders, to hold councils as to what quarters they should march, and they said among-themselves, that though the kings had made peace with each other, it was necessary for them to live. They marched into Burgundy, where they had captains of all nations, Germans, Scots, and people from every country. I was there also as a captain. Our numbers in Burgundy, above the river Loire, were upwards of twelve thousand, including all sorts; but I must say, that in this number, there were three or four thousand good men at arms, as able and understanding in war as any could be found, whether to plan an engagement, to seize a proper moment to fight, or to surprise and scale towns and castles, and well inured to war; which indeed we showed at the battle of Brignais, where we overpowered the constable of France, the count de Forêts, with full two thousand lances, knights, and squires.

"This battle was of great advantage to the companions, for they were poor, and they then enriched themselves by good prisoners, and by the towns and castles which they took in the archbishopric of Lyons on the river Rhone. They carried on their warfare until they had gained the Pont du St. Esprit: and the pope and cardinals would not have been freed from them until they had destroyed everything, if they had not thought of a good expedient, by sending to Lombardy for the marquis de Montferrat, who was a gallant knight, and at that time at war with the lord of Milan. On his arrival at Avignon, the pope and cardinals had a conference with him: and he negotiated with the English, Gascon, and German troops for their services, for sixty thousand francs, which the pope and cardinals paid to different leaders of these companies; such as sir John Hawkwood, a valiant English knight, sir Robert Bricquet, Carsuelle, Naudon le Bagerant, le bourg Camus, and many more.

"They marched into Lombardy, having surrendered the Pont du St; Esprit, and carried with them six parts of the companies; but sir Sequin de Batefol, sir John Jewel, sir James Planchin, sir John Amery, le bourg de Perigord, Espiote, Louis Raimbaut, Limousin, James Trittel, and myself, with several others, remained behind. We had possession of Ance, St. Clement, la Barrelle, la Terrare, Brignais, le Pont St. Denis, l'Hopital d'Ortifart, and upwards of sixty castles in the Maconnois, Forêts, Velay, and in lower Burgundy on the Loire. We ransomed the whole country, and they could only be freed from us by well paying. We took, by a night-attack, la Charité, which we held for a year and a half. Everything was ours from la Charité to Puy in Auvergne (for sir Sequin de Batefol had left Ance, and resided at Brioude in Auvergne, where he made great profit, and gained there and in the adjacent country upwards of one hundred thousand francs), and below Loire as far as Orleans, with the command of the whole river Allier.

"The archpriest, who was then a good Frenchman, and governor of Nevers, could not remedy this; but, being our old acquaintance, we sometimes complied with his entreaties to spare the country. The archpriest did great good to the Nivernois, by fortifying the city of Nevers, which otherwise would have been ruined several times; for we had in the environs upwards of twenty-six strong places, as well towns as castles, and no knight, squire, nor rich man, dared to quit his home unless he had compounded with us; and this war we carried on under the name and pretext of the king of Navarre. At this time happened the battle of Cocherel, where the captal de Buch commanded for the king of Navarre, and many knights and squires went from us to assist him: sir James Planchin and sir John Jewel carried with them two hundred lances. I held at this period a castle called le Bee d'Allier, pretty near to la Charité, on the road to the Bourbonnois, and had under me forty lances, where I made great profit from the country near Moulins, and about St. Pourpain and St. Pierre le Moustier.

"When news was brought me that the captal, my master, was in Constantin, collecting men from all parts, having a great desire to see him, I left my castle with twelve lances, with whom I joined sir James Planchin and sir John Jewel, and without accident or adventure we came to the captal. I believe you must have all this in your history, as well as the event of the battle."

"Yes, I have," said I: "how the captal was made prisoner, and sir James Planchin and sir John Jewel killed."

"That is right," added he: "I also was made prisoner; but good luck befell me, for it was to my cousin: he was cousin to my cousin now by my side the bourg de Copaire; and his name was Bernard de Turide: he was killed in Portugal, at the affair of Aljubarrota. Bernard, then under the command of sir Aymemon de Pommiers, ransomed me in the field for a thousand francs, and gave me a passport to return to my fort of Bee d'Alliers. Instantly on my arrival, I counted out to one of my servants a thousand francs, which I charged him to carry to Paris, and to bring me back letters of acquittance for the payment, which he did.

"At this same season, sir John Aymery, an English knight, and the greatest captain we had, made an excursion down the Loire towards la Charité: he fell into an ambuscade of the lords de Rougement and de Vendelay, with the men of the archpriest. They were the strongest, and overpowered him: he was made prisoner, and ransomed for thirty thousand francs which he instantly paid down. He was, however, so much vexed at being captured, and with his loss that he swore he would never re-enter his fort until he had had his revenge. He collected, therefore, a large body of companions, and came to la Charité on the Loire, and. entreated the captains, such as Lamit, Carsuelle, le bourg de Perigord, and myself (who were come thither for our amusement), to accompany him in an expedition.

"We asked him, Whither?'

"By my faith," replied he, "we will cross the Loire at port St. Thibaut, and scale the town and castle of Sancerre. I have made a vow, that I will never re-enter my own castle until I shall have seen the boys of Sancerre; and if we could conquer that garrison, with the earl's children within it, John Louis and Robert, we should be made men, and masters of the whole country. We may easily succeed in our attempt, for they pay no attention to us, and our remaining longer here is not of any advantage."

"That is true," we answered, and promised to accompany him, and went away to make ourselves ready.

"It happened," continued le Bascot de Mauléon, "that our plot was discovered, and known in the town of Sancerre. A valiant squire from the lower parts of Burgundy, called Guichart d'Albigon, was at the time governor of the town, who took great pains to guard it well. The earl's children, who were all three knights, were with him. This Guichart had a brother a monk in the abbey of St. Thibaut near Sancerre, who was sent by the governor to in Charité with the composition-money that some of the towns in the upper districts owed. They were careless about him, and he discovered, I know not how, our intentions and what our numbers were, as well as the names of the captains of the different forts near in Charité, with the strength of their garrisons, and also at what hour and in what manner we were to cross the river at Port St. Thibaut.

"Having gained this information, he hastened to disclose it to his brother and the young knights of Sancerre. They made instant preparations for their defence, and sent notice of the, intended attack to the knights and squires of Berry and the Bourbonnois, and to the captains of the different garrisons in the neighbourhood, so that they were four hundred good lances. They placed a strong ambuscade, of two hundred spears, in a wood near to the town.

"We set out at sun-set from la Charité, and rode on briskly, in good order, until we came to Prully, where we had collected a number of boats, to pass us and our horses over the river. We crossed the Loire, as we had intended, and were all over about midnight: our horses crossed, also, without accident; but, as day-break was near, we ordered a hundred of our men to remain behind, to guard the horses and boats; and the rest advanced with a good pace, passing by the ambuscade, which took no notice of us. When we had gone about a quarter of a league, they sallied forth upon those at the river side, whom they instantly conquered; for all were slain or made prisoners; the horses were captured, and the passage of the river secured, when, mounting our horses, they stuck spurs into them, and arrived at the town as soon as we did.

"They shouted on all sides, "Our lady for Sancerre!" for the count himself was in the town with his men, and sir Louis and sir Robert had formed the ambuscade. We were thus completely surrounded, and knew not which way to turn ourselves: the shock of lances was great; for those on horseback instantly dismounted on their arrival, and attacked us fiercely; but what hurt us the most was the impossibility of extending our front, for we were enclosed in a narrow road, with hedges and vineyards on ends side, with our enemies before and behind us. They knew well the country, and had posted a body of their men and servants in the vineyards, who cast stones and flints that bruised us much : we could not retreat, and had also great difficulty to approach the town, which is situated on a bill.

"We had very hard work: sir John Aymery, our captain, who had led us thither, was dangerously wounded by Guichart d'Albigon, who, exerting himself to save him, pushed him into a house in the town, and threw him on a bed, telling the master to take great care of his prisoner, and make haste to have his wounds dressed, for his rank was such, that if his life were saved, he would pay twenty thousand francs. On saying this, Guichart left his prisoner and returned to the battle, where he showed himself a good man at arms.

"Among others, the young knights of Sancerre had come to defend the country, with sir Guichard Dauphin, the lord de Marnay, sir Gerard and sir William de Bourbon, the lords de Cousant, de la Pierre, de la Palice, de Neutey, de la Croise, de la Sicete, and many more; I must say it was a very hard-fought

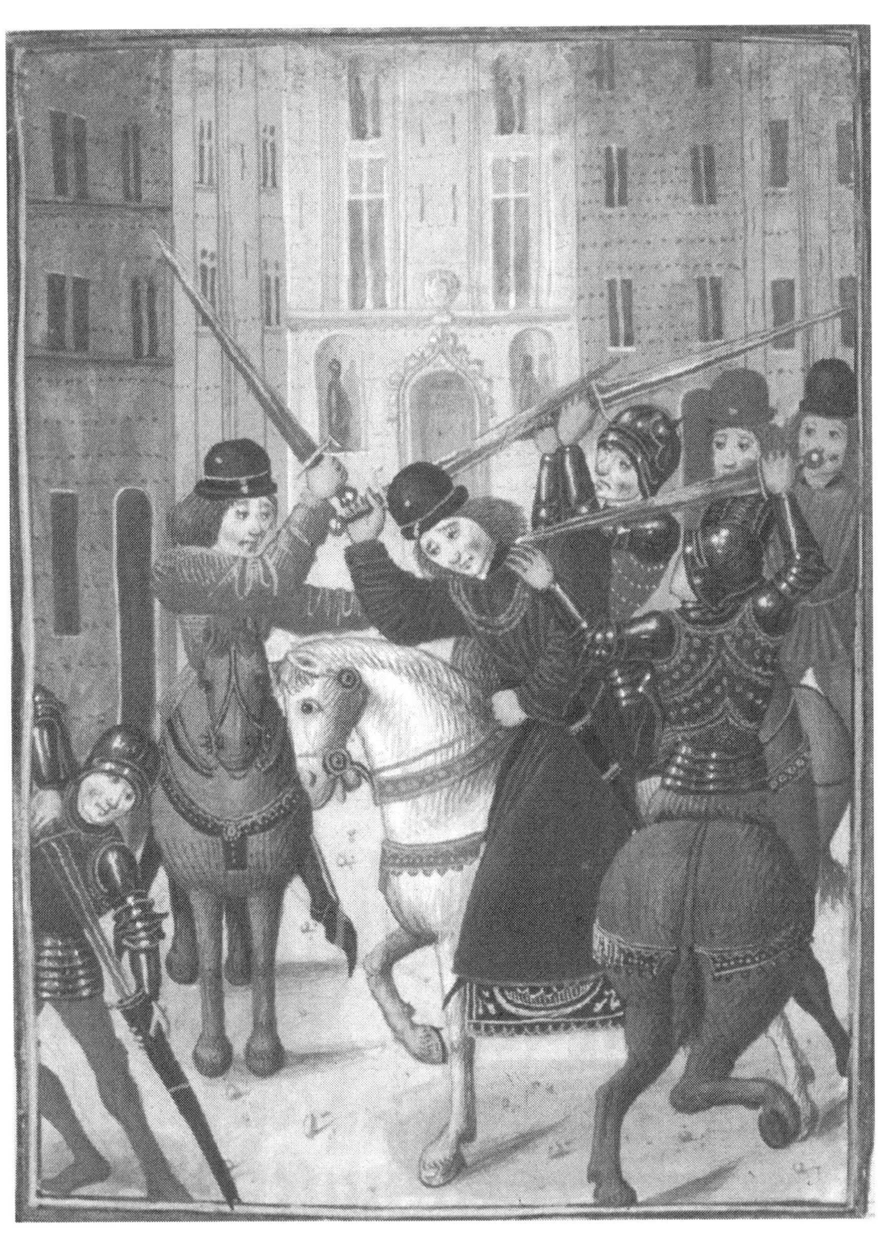

Attack on Olivier de Clisson by followers of Pierre de Craon. (British Library, Harley 4379 f. 152v)

murderous battle; we kept our ground as long as we were able, insomuch that several were slain and wounded on both sides.

"By their actions they seemed more desirous to take us alive than to kill us: at last they made prisoners of Carsuelle, Lamit Naudon le bourg de Perigord, le bourg de l'Esparre, Angerot, Lamontgis, Philip du Roe, Pierre de Corthon, le Pesat de Pamiers, le bourg d'Armesen; in short, all our companions who were in that neighbourhood. We were conducted to the castle of Sancerre in great triumph: and the free companies never suffered such loss in France as they did that day. Guichart d'Albigon, however, lost his prisoner through negligence, for he bled so much that he died: such was the end of John Aymery.

"By this defeat, which happened under the wails of Sancerre, la Charité sur Loire surrendered to the French, as well as all the garrisons thereabout, by which means we obtained our liberties, and had passports given us to quit the kingdom of France and go whithersoever we pleased. Fortunately for us, sir Bertrand du Guesclin, the lord de Beaujen, sir Arnold d'Andreghen, and the count de la Marche, at this moment undertook an expedition into Spain, to assist the bastard Henry against don Pedro.

"Before that time, I was in Brittany at the battle of Auraye, where I served under sir Hugh Calverley, and recovered my affairs; for the day was ours, and I made such good prisoners, they paid me two thousand francs. I accompanied sir Hugh Calverley with ten lances into Spain, when we drove from thence don Pedro; but when treaties were afterwards made between don Pedro and the prince of Wales, who wished to enter Castille, I was there, in the company of sir Hugh Calverley, and returned to Aquitaine with him.

"The war was now renewed between the king of France and the prince: we had enough to do, for it was vigorously carried on; and great numbers of English and Gascon commanders lost their lives: however, thanks to God, I am still alive. Sir Robert Briquet was slain at a place called Olivet, in the Orleannois, situated between the territories of the duke of Orleans and the country of Blois, where a squire from Hainault, a gallant man at arms, and good captain, called Alars de Doustiennes, surnamed de Barbazan, for he was of that family, met him, and conquered both him and his company. This Alars was at that time governor of Blois and its dependencies, for the lords Lewis, John, and Guy de Blois; and it chanced that he met sir Robert Briquet and sir Robert Cheney at Olivet, when both were slain on the spot, and all their men, for none were ransomed. Afterwards, at time battle of Niort, Carsuelie was killed by sir Bertrand du Guesclin, and seven hundred English perished that day. Richard Ellis and Richard Heline, two English captains, were also killed at St. Severe: I know but few, except myself who have escaped death.

"I have guarded the frontiers, and supported the king of England; for my estate is in the Bordelois; and I have at times been so miserably poor that I had not a horse to mount, at other times rich enough, just as good fortune befell me.

"Raymonet de l'Espee and I were some time companions: we held the castles of Mauvoisin, Trigalet, and Nantilleux, in the Toulousain, on the borders of Bigorre, which were very profitable to us. When the duke of Anjon came to attack them with his army, Raymonet turned to the French; but I remained steady to the English, and shall do so as long as I live. In truth, when I lost the castle of Trigalet, and was escorted to castle Cuillet, after the retreat of the duke of Anjon into France, I resolved to do something which should either make me or ruin me. I therefore sent spies to reconnoitre the town and castle of Thurie in the Aibigeois, which castle has since been worth to me, as well by compositions as by good luck, one hundred thousand francs. I will tell you by what means I conquered it.

"On the outside of the town and castle, there is a beautiful spring of water, where every morning the women of the town come to fill their pails or other vessels; which having done, they carry them back on their heads. Upon this, I formed my plan; and, taking with me fifty men from the castle of Cuillet, we rode all day over heaths and through woods, and about midnight I placed an ambuscade near Thurie. Myself, with only six others, disguised as women, with pails in our hands, entered the meadow very near the town, and hid ourselves in a heap of hay; for it was about St. John's day, and the meadows were mown and making into hay.

"When the usual hour of opening the gates arrived, and the women were coming to the fountain, each of us then took his pail, and having filled it placed it on his head, and made for the town, our faces covered with handkerchiefs so that no one could have known us. The women that met us, said, "Holy Mary, how early must you have risen this morning!" We replied in feigned voices, and passed on to the gate, where we found no other guard but a cobler, who was mending shoes. One of us sounded his horn, as a notice for the ambuscade to advance. The cobler, who had not paid any attention to us, on hearing the horn, cried out, "Hola! who is it that has blown the horn?" We answered, "It is a priest who is going into the country: I know not whether he be the curate or chaplain of the town." "That is true," replied he: "it is sir Francis, our priest, who likes to go early to the fields in search of hares."

"Our companions soon joined us, when we entered the town and found no one prepared to defend it. Thus did I gain the town and castle of Thurie, which has been to me of greater profit and more annual revenue than this castle and all its dependencies are worth. At this moment, I know not how to act: for I am in treaty with the count d'Armagnac and the dauphin d'Auvergne, who have been expressly commissioned by the king of France to buy all towns and castles from the captains of the free companies, wherever they may be, in Auvergne, Rouergue, Limousin, Agen, Quercy, Perigord, Albigeois, and from all those who have made war under the name of the king of England. Several have sold their forts, and gone away; and I am doubtful whether or not to sell mine."

Upon this, the bourg de Copaire said, "Cousin, what you say is true; for I also have had intelligence since my arrival at Orthès, from Carlet, which I hold in Auvergne, that the lord Louis de Sancerre, marshal of France, will soon be here: he is now incognito at Tarbes, as I have heard from those who have seen him."

They now called for wine, of which when brought we all drank, and Bascot de Mauléon said to me, "Well, sir John, what do you say ? Have I well told you my life? I have had many more adventures, but of which I neither can nor will speak." "Yes, that you have, by my faith," added I: and, wishing him to continue his conversation, I asked what was become of a gallant squire, called Louis Raimbaut, whom I had met once at Avignon.

"I will tell you," replied he. "At the time when sir Sequin de Batefol, who had possession of Brioude in Vélay, ten leagues from Pay in Auvergne, after having carried on the war in that country with much success, was returning to Gascony, he gave to Louis Raimbaut and to a companion of his, called Limousin, Brioude and Ance on the Saone. The country at that time was so desolated and harassed, and so full of free companies in every part, that none dared to venture out of their houses. I must inform you, that between Brioude and

Ance, the country is mountainous, and the distance from one of those towns to the other twenty-six leagues.

"However, when Louis Raimbaut was pleased to ride from one of these places to the other, he made nothing of it; for he had several forts in Forêts and elsewhere, to halt and refresh himself. The gentlemen of Auvergue, Forêts, and Velay, had been so oppressed by ransoms to regain their liberty, they dreaded to take up arms again; and there were no great lords in France who raised any men. The king of France was young, and had too much to do in various parts of his kingdom; for the free companies had quartered themselves everywhere, and he could not get rid of them. Many of the great lords of France were hostages in England; during which time their property and vassals were pillaged, and there was not any remedy for this mischief, as their men were too dispirited even to defend themselves.

"Louis Raimbaut and Limousin, who had been brothers in arms, at length. quarrelled, and I will tell you why. Louis Raimbaut had at Brioude a very handsome woman for his mistress, of whom he was passionately fond; and, when he made any excursions from Brioude to Ance, he intrusted her to the care of Limousin. Limousin was his brother in arms, and in him did he put his whole confidence; but he took such good care of the fair lady that he obtained every favour from her, and Louis Raimbaut had information of it. This enraged Louis Raimbaut against his companion; and, in order to insult him as much as possible, he ordered him to be seized by his servants and marched naked, all but his drawers, through the town, and then flogged with rods: at every corner of a street, trumpets sounded before him, and his action was proclaimed: he was then, in this state, and with only a plain coat on, thrust out of the town, and banished as a traitor.

"Louis Raimbaut thus insulted Limousin; but he was so much

hurt at it, he vowed revenge whenever he should have an opportunity, which he afterwards found. Limousin, during the time he was in command at Brioude, had always spared the lands of the lord de la Voulte, situated on the Rhône, in his different excursions to Ance, and in the country of Vélay, for he had been kind to him in his youth. He therefore resolved to go to him, entreat his mercy, and beg he would make his peace with France, for that he would henceforward be a loyal Frenchman. He went therefore to Voulte, being well acquainted with the roads, and entered a house, for he was on foot: after he had inquired what hour it was, he went to the castle to wait on its lord.

"The porter would not at first allow him to enter the gate; but, after many fair words, he was permitted to come into the gateway, and ordered not to stir further without permission, which he cheerfully promised. The lord de la Voulte, in the afternoon, came into the court to amuse himself, and advanced to the gate: Limousin instantly cast himself on his knees, and said, "My lord, do you not know me?"

"Not I, by my faith," replied the lord, who never imagined it was Limousin; but, having looked at him some time, added: "Thou resemblest very much Limousin, who was formerly my page."

"On my troth, my lord, Limousin I am, and your servant also." he then begged his pardon for what had passed, and told him exactly everything that had happened to him, and how Louis Raimbaut had treated him.

"The lord de la Voulte said, "Limousin, if what thou hast told me be true, and if I may rely on thy assurance that thou wilt become a good Frenchman, I will make thy peace."

"By my faith, my lord, I have never done so much harm to

France as I will from henceforward do it service." 'I shall see,' replied the lord de la Voulte.

From that time he retained him in his castle, and did not allow him to depart until he had made his peace everywhere. When Limousin could with honour bear arms, the lord de la Voulte mounted and armed him, and conducted him to the séneschal de Vélay, at Puy, to make them acquainted with each other. He was there examined as to the strength and situation of Brioude, and also respecting Louis Raimbaut; at what times he made excursions, and whither he generally directed them. I know by heart the roads he takes, for with him and without him I have too often traversed them; and, if you will collect a body of men at arms for an expedition, I will forfeit my head if you do not take him within a fortnight."

"The lords agreed to his proposal, and spies were sent abroad to observe when Louis Raimbaut should leave Brioude for Ance in the Lyonois. When Limousin was certain he had left Brioude, he told the lord de la Voulte to assemble his men, for that Raimbaut was at Ance and would soon return, and that he would conduct them to a defile through which he must pass. The lord de la Voulte collected his men, and made him the leader of the expedition, having sent off to the bailiff of Vélay, the lord de Montelare, sir Guerrot de Salieres, and his son, sir Plouserat de Vernot, the lord de Villeneuve, and to all the men at arms thereabout: they were in the whole full three hundred spears; and when assembled at Nonnay, by the advice of Limousin, they formed two ambuscades. The viscount de Polignac and the lord de Chalençon commanded one, and the lords de la Voulte, de Montelare, de Salieres, and sir Louis de Tournon, the other. They had equally divided their men; and the viscount de Polignac and his party were posted near St. Rambut in Foi{ts, at a pass where Louis Raimbaut would be forced to cross the river Loire at the bridge, or higher up at a ford above Puy.

"When Louis Raimbaut had finished his business at Ance, he set out with forty lances; not expecting to meet with any one, nor suspecting anything from Limousin, as he was the farthest from his thoughts. I must tell you, that he was accustomed never to go and return by the same road: he had come by St. Rambut. On his return, he went over the hills above Lyons, and Vienne, and below the village of Argental, and then straight towards le Monastier, three short leagues from Puy; and, after passing between the castles of Menestrol and Montfaucon, he made a circuit towards a village called le Batterie, between Nonnay and St. Julien.

"There is a pass in the wood there that cannot be avoided by any of those who take this road, unless they go through Nonnay; and there was posted the ambuscade of the lord de la Voulte, with about two hundred spears. Louis Raimbaut, suspecting nothing, was surprised; and the lord de la Voulte and his men, knowing what they were to do, lowered their lances, and, shouting their cry of "La Voulte!" instantly charged him and his companions, who were riding much at their ease. On the first shock, the greater part were unhorsed: and Louis Raimbaut was struck to the ground by a squire of Auvergne, called Amblardon, who, advancing on him, made him his prisoner; the remainder were either killed or taken; not one escaped; and they found in a private trunk the sum of three thousand francs, which he had received at Ance as the composition of the villagers near, which gave much pleasure to the captors, for each had a share.

"When Limousin saw Louis Raimbaut thus caught, he showed himself, and said reproachfully, "Louis, Louis! you should have been better accompanied. Do you remember the insult and shame you made me undergo at Brioude, on account of your mistress? I did not think that for a woman you would have made me suffer what you did; for, if it had happened to me, I should not have been so angry. To two brothers in arms, such as we were then, one woman might have occasionally served."

"The lords laughed at this speech, but Louis had no such inclination. By the capture of Louis Raimbaut, those of Brioude surrendered to the séneschal of Auvergne; for, after the loss of their leader and the flower of their men, they could not keep it. The garrisons at Ance and in the other forts in Vélay and Forêts did the same, and were glad to escape with their lives. Louis Raimbaut was carried to Nonnay and imprisoned: information was sent the king of France of the event, who was much rejoiced thereat; and soon after, as I have heard, orders came for him to be beheaded at Villeneuve, near Avignon. Thus died Louis Raimbaut: may God receive his soul!

"Now, my fair sir" said Bascot de Mauléon, "have not I well chatted away the night? and yet all I have said is true."

"Indeed you have," answered I, "and many thanks for it: I have had great pleasure in listening to you, and it shall not be lost; for, if God permit me to return to my own country, all I have heard you say, and all I shall have seen worthy to be mentioned, in the noble and grand history which the gallant count de Blois has employed me on, shall be chronicled, through God's grace, that the memory of such events may be perpetuated."

On saying this, the bourg de Copaire, whose name was Ernauton, began to speak, and, I could perceive, would willingly have related the life and adventures of himself and his brother, the bourg Anglois; and how they had borne arms in Auvergne and elsewhere, but there was not time; for the watch of the castle had sounded his horn, to assemble those in the town of Orthès, who were engaged to sup with the count de Foix. The two squires then made themselves ready, and, having lighted torches, we left the inn together, taking the road to the castle, as did all the knights and squires who lodged in the town.

Too much praise cannot be given to the state and magnificence of the count de Foix, nor can it be too much recommended; for, during my stay there, I found him such, as far to exceed all that I can say of him, and I saw many things which gave me great pleasure.

About **Tales from Froissart**
This series continues a long tradition of making Froissart's Chronicles available to a wide readership. The various excerpts are taken from Thomas Johnes' 1805 English translation, which is still the most complete English version of Froissart's histories.

About **Steven Muhlberger**
Dr. Muhlberger, formerly of Nipissing University in North Bay, Ontario, has taught (among other things) medieval history, Islamic history, and the history of world democracy. He has a particular interest in military history and the history of chivalry in the later Middle Ages, and has written extensively on those topics.

A complete listing of Dr. Muhlberger's scholarly books can be found at Steve Muhlberger's Books (smuhlberger.weebly.com)

History of Chivalry
From Freelance Academy Press (freelanceacademypress.com):
- *Jousts and Tournaments*
- *Deeds of Arms*
- *Charny's Men- at-Arms*
- The *Deeds of Arms* series (accounts of chivalric feats)

From Witan Publishing (www.witanpublishing.com):
- *Formal Combats in the Fourteenth Century*

Made in the USA
Lexington, KY
03 June 2016